THE QUEST FOR BELIEF
A STUDY OF THE NOVELS OF THEODORE DREISER

Hemalatha Iyer

RAJAT PUBLICATIONS
New Delhi

The Quest for Belief: A Study of the Novels of Theodore Dreiser
by *Hemalatha Iyer*

This edition is published by Rajat Publications
4740/23, Ansari Road Daryaganj,
New Delhi - 110002

ISBN: 978-81-7880-252-7

Edition 2025
Rs. 1695/-

Printed and bound in India

RAJAT
PUBLICATIONS

4740/23, Ansari Road, Daryaganj,
New Delhi- 110002 (India)
Mob:- +91-9811484973, +91-9811105389
E-mail: rajat_publication@yahoo.com

Dedicated

to

MY PARENTS

FOREWORD

The question of 'who am I' has been addressed by man from time immemorial and every individual at different phases of his life has responded to this in his own experiential manner. Literature has provided a wide canvas to explore this phenomenon and many writers have explored this in their writings. Theodore Dreiser, the renowned American writer, who made his mark with his famous novels *Sister Carrie*, *Jennie Gerhardt* and an *American Tragedy*, has similarly left tell tale marks of his spiritual growth in the course of his novels. Dreiser has explored the mystery of life and has evolved a belief in the universal truth of *Aham Brahmaśmi*- the unifying principle of universal kinship or universal brotherhood.

What impressed me about the book is the fact that Theodore Dreiser , who lived in America at the time when the American Quest for Wealth was at its peak- the age of money barons- the Rockefellers, the Carnegies, the Vanderbilts, humbly rejects the idea of wealth accumulation and turns to India for spiritual solace and enlightenment.

Dreiser's novels reveal that if one individual emerges to be strong , powerful and manipulating with accumulation of wealth, then collectively he can be crushed by society which can overpower him. If Capitalism is a failure, Communism which does not practice what it preaches is also a failure. So according to Dreiser the only solution to America's giddiness in wealth acquisition is to return to the world of spirituality, learn to establish 'Oneness' with nature , 'Cosmic Consciousness' with the Universe and thrive on an atmosphere of universal love, humanism and wholehearted service to society.

Man made laws demarcate humans as saints and sinners, whereas God's glory encompasses not only all humans but all creations on earth -for instance a snake which happened to cross his pathway seems to be an embodiment of cosmic beauty in all its glory and delight, thereby revealing the message that God is manifest as the smallest of small and largest of large atoms or forms:- *Anudwena mahatwena dwitha dishtati keshava.*

In the book Dr. Hemalatha has dealt with the various stages of experiences in life which lead to the spiritual transformation of Theodore Dreiser from being an agnostic to one of believer. In the first chapter she has dealt with the condition of America in which Dreiser was born, his family background and the various literary movements present during his time. While trying to explore the purpose of his writings, she has explained Dreiser's inclination towards Naturalism, Realism and Darwinism.

The second chapter is a detailed analysis of Dreiser's *Sister Carrie* and *Jennie Gerhardt.* In these novels Dreiser's search for a "theory of existence"and the way in which the protagonists in these novels struggle for social ascendance and escape from poverty has been explicitly delineated. The third chapter while dealing with the Darwinian theory of "Survival of the Fittest" as portrayed by Dreiser in his trilogy, *The Financier* , *The Titan* and *The Stoic,* reveals the struggle between the masses and a powerful individual — a Superman, and his ultimate realization of the futility of the effort to amass wealth and power.

The fourth chapter exposes an artist's struggle to choose between art and a lucrative career in business in the novel *The "Genius"* and other short stories of his. The clash between biological and social determinism and the fierce nature of the social struggle, which leaves the individual physically and morally weak and therefore no longer capable of any productive work, has been lucidly elaborated.

The fifth chapter is also a discussion of the role of social and biological determinism which results in the tragedy of a young man in *An American Tragedy.* Dreiser's leaning towards Communism as a solution to the problems of America has also been analyzed. The sixth chapter deals with the gradual emergence of Dreiser's theory of existence and the seventh chapter sums up Dreiser's " Quest for Belief."

In the concluding chapter Dr. Hemalatha has brought out

parallels from the *Gita* and Dreiser's philosophy as expressed in his novels. It is also heartening to note that Theodore Dreiser used to carry a copy of the *Bhagavad Gita* with him. In her study Dr.Hemalatha has pointed out how Dreiser was actually looking for a scheme behind the apparent schemelessness or chaotic appearance of the universe , and how ultimately he came to understand that selflessness, admiration of Beauty and appreciation and acceptance of the unity in the scheme of things is what life is all about. She has highlighted the fact that Dreiser's novels are a wake-up call for humanity to wake up, give up meanness , establish a oneness with Nature, and with a magnanimous and philanthropic mind, be ready to help others in distress. This spirit of "Oneness" shall bring about Universal peace, Contentment and a sense of accomplishment and fulfillment in society.

Dr. Hemalatha has made an in-depth study of Dreiser's novels and systematically analyzed his works to explore the gradual development of Dreiser's quest for a meaning of life and how he finally arrived at it from his readings of Vedic Philosophy and *The Gita.* It is delightful to note that like other American writers Thoreau, Emerson and Whitman, Dreiser has also done India proud by projecting it on the world map of Spirituality. I wish Dr. Hemalatha Good Luck and God Speed.

Prof. Swatantra Kumar

Vice Chancellor

Gurukul Kangri Vishwavidyalaya,

Haridwar

PREFACE

Theodore Dreiser has an acclaimed place in American literature. His novels *Sister Carrie, Jennie Gerhardt* and *An American Tragedy* have been highlighting the condition of society along with its weaknesses and myths. As far as criticism is concerned, critics have carefully observed and analysed Dreiser's interest in Naturalism, Social Darwinism, Determinism and Realism, and have slotted him as a realist, naturalist and so on.

At a deeper, more profound level, what struck me was the gradual development of another powerful theme in the course of Dreiser's novels -his Quest For Belief. Questioning the disparity between man's desires and his ultimate accomplishment, Dreiser almost arrived at a solution to the mystery which confounded him. This enabled him to frame his ideology and establish his fervent belief in the Just, Intelligent, Loving and Supremely Resourceful and Powerful Force or Law or Being which creates and carries the universe on towards its destiny. The present study is therefore an attempt to trace the development of his thoughts through various stages until finally he arrives at the solution towards the end of his career, with the publication of *The Bulwark*.

As a novelist, Dreiser limited himself most sternly, to what he knew of life through his own experiences. His inner struggles and mental torments provided him with one of the chief motifs of his fiction: the conflict between what was then loosely termed "instinct" by psychologists. Frequently he calls these impulses as "Chemisms". Man acting in accordance with the natural impulse, seeks to satisfy himself.Of all the most imaginative and creative American novelists, Theodore Dreiser is one of the most thoughtful and intellectual. Often called the pioneer of naturalism in American fiction, he is equally admired for his vigorous attack on the genteel tradition and his long, active and fervent interest in American social problems. Dreiser's publications between the years 1922-1931 reveal his early confusion and his struggles to find a satisfactory pattern for life. Dreiser displayed unique skill in realism which was almost photographic. He insisted that the writer as a clinician of the forces of nature, must report life as he saw it and. therefore must have the freedom to do so. According to Robert E. Spillers. Dreiser "reveals the very nerves of American society. He has exerted a more profound, a most lasting influence than any other novelist on twentieth century realistic fiction in America. Several generations of writers are already his debtors. His influence is seen in a seriousness of approach to the material of American life, in a greater freedom of theme,in the parallelism of ideas and phenomenon. Dreiser described the broad patterns of modern American experience... he was faithful to his art and made no compromises...his work gives a sense of totality and finality."

Dreiser was an objective realist who gathered his facts impersonally. He absorbed the naturalistic understanding of life, the realistic method and the new conceptions of the universe from science into his thoughts and writings. His views are loose in formulation but his theory of relativity of morals is quite challenging. Dreiser's views on man and nature contributed to the feeling of awe he creates concerning the condition of man; they served him in his very construction of theme, of story, of character. Though endowed with a firm , ciear and intense ideological attitude, he was only an artist and not a philosopher.

Dreiser believed that life as a quest for power, an effort to express creativity becomes a struggle, for money and position and for instinctual satisfaction, on the plane of society. In this quest and rivalry, the strongest win out; the weak are crushed. Thus to biological is added social determinism. As the stronger man has an advantage over the weaker, so organised groups are stronger than the individual. Explicating this equation further, Dreiser found that the poor are the victims of the rich, the weak of the strong and women are victims of men. Therefore *American Tragedy* like all tragedy is the result of weakness. The impulses, the passions of man pitilessly drive him to satisfy himself; the force of social circumstances, the fierce nature of the social struggle, thwart him and produce both social and biological tragedy.

Dreiser has observed the customs and class structure of American society, in the early phase of capitalization of America. With America marching towards industrialization and urbanization, the "American Dream of Success" , had spread its tentacles far and wide entrapping many young Americans in its powerful grip. Great money-barons like Rockefellers, Carnegies and Rogers were ruling over America manipulating, crushing competitors and grabbing the lion's share of profit.

So in the 1890's there was a change in the outlook in society, which was ready to sacrifice the old Puritan values of simplicity and honesty, and join the main stream in Deifying, worshipping and emulating the life style of money-barons. Money, worldly success and sensual gratification seemed to be their sole prerogatives. There was class consciousness and the fear of poverty served as a driving force. The people struggled hard and diverted all their energy to ascend the ladder of success. Such misguided energies lead to chaos and turmoil and the whole society appeared like a jungle, with all men giving vent to their innate instincts, without any pricking of conscience or moral binding whatsoever. Americans were vying with one another to reach the top, trampling weaker ones underfoot. Such craze for wealth had worked havoc in the lives of many a young American.

Dreiser was depressed to view such a state of affairs, and so wished to delve deeper and discover the mystery of life on earth. The only method which Dreiser adopted to solve the mystery was by observing and recording incidents or influences which he had in life. Thus in the first two novels *Sister Carrie* (1900) and *Jennie Gerhardt* (1911). Dreiser made bold to reveal the stories of "fallen" women in an age when the readers felt that it was blasphemous even to mention such topics. Dreiser actually went one step further in rewarding a "fallen woman" with material success in *Sister Carrie.* Here, what Dreiser was trying to do was to make explicit the fact that men and women do not always suffer in this life for transgressions of the social and moral code.

Therefore we find that Dreiser's characters are placed in a pre- determined universe. A portion of their fate is determined by society, and another portion by forces beyond them, and the characters grope in the dark until eventually they reach their destiny. This apparent helplessness of man in the face of inscrutable laws of fate and nature was what troubled Dreiser in the initial stage of his career as a novelist.

The formation of trusts and corporations and the sudden growth of stock markets, made many people invest crazily in stocks and shares. The craze was so strong that people borrowed money from banks and invested it in stocks and shares. This resulted in the creation of a few powerful men who manipulated the stocks to their own advantage and became millionaires very soon. Dreiser's trilogy *The Financier* (1912),*The Titan(*1914) and *The Stoic(*1947) have recorded such observations of his.

This made Dreiser think deeply as to what would be the outcome of such craze for instant success. It was then that Dreiser was also seized upon by Darwin's theory of "Survival of the Fittest" and so he almost came to believe that only the fittest could survive. During Dreiser's literary career, Social Darwinism was the main current of American thought. Its central concept was the equation of nature with society. It conceived the natural and the social worlds as continuous, subsumable to the same laws; in consequence, it attempted to give the status of social generalization the conclusion of biological evolution. Dreiser accepting this fact, developed from it an attitude of both personal and social determinism. Man is for him a creature with imperious biological needs. The "instincts" drive him to actions whose motivation he does not understand. For Dreiser the view that only the fittest could survive did not last long, as his observations revealed to him the fact that if an individual becomes powerful, then there are others in society ready to crush and defeat him and usurp his place.

Dreiser did not have any faith or belief in institutionalized religion which could not actually help the downtrodden, underprivileged people. Religion and morals to Dreiser are a matter of convenience. Religion according to Dreiser should relate to the world as a whole and not in bits and parts.It is unjustified for man to form laws and brand anyone as being amoral or immoral. All such norms are not permanent and so are bound to change. They change with a change in society's views and style of living. Therefore we find that in the novels of Dreiser the most powerful character is society. Society can make or break families by way of slanderous talk, or by recording and spreading rumours in newspapers or by uniting to crush and defeat strong and powerful individuals.

In the novel *An American Tragedy (*1925) Dreiser has portrayed how the values of society shape Clyde Griffith's tawdry ambitions to culminate in murder and ultimately seal his fate. The novel is an unsurpassed depiction of harsh realities of American life and the dark side of the American dream. If the whole society had believed in a life of simplicity and honesty then Clyde would not have met with such a fate.

Dreiser had then thought of Socialism as a solution to America's problems, but later on decided against it, as he felt that nothing much could be achieved, as Communism does not practise what it preaches. According to Dreiser, capitalism was also a failure because the common man was seen nowhere in the picture. The best way of describing Dreiser's total literary work would be to state that he was engaged in a life long search for a "theory of existence". Dreiser, a voracious reader himself, read Hindu and Buddhist Philosophy, with a complete lack of bias, and a keen desire to know the truth behind the scheme of life and its affairs. *The Gita* and *The Upanishads* afforded Dreiser with an in-depth knowledge of the mystery of the universe.

Dreiser's philosophy of life is comparable to that of the transcendentalists, Emerson, Thoreau and Whitman who also proclaimed a "Oneness" with Nature and established a "Cosmic Consciousness" with the universe. This Universe including the social world of man, is all one piece, a product of unknown force, creative by nature and resident in human organisms. The impulses in man are also expressions of some unapprehended force, or energy, purpose, or "God " in the universe.

Dreiser framed his ideology and opinion that the Equation Inevitable would definitely take place, setting things right and the balance in society would definitely be maintained. *The Stoic* which is the third and last part of his trilogy, has confirmed Dreiser's faith in a Powerful Force or Law or Being which leads the universe towards its destiny. In *The Bulwark* (1946) Solon Barnes the protagonist relies on an "Inner Light" and averts the danger of being bit by a poisonous snake by looking at it with the eyes of love. So Dreiser reveals that universal love is the Guiding Force which takes us along.

Thus we find that in the course of his novels, Dreiser has graduated from the purposelessness of existence on earth to the realization and belief that as souls are eternal, our existence on earth is also eternal. Identifying God and soul as being one and the same, Dreiser was able to perceive Supreme Bliss when one lived in harmony with Nature.

Dreiser novels are a revelation and a call to fellow Americans to avoid being over indulgent in material comforts but to rise up, unite and work for the uplift of humanity as such. If great Financiers could give up their craftiness, cruelty, avarice, greed and self-centredness and care for the deprived and down trodden then the whole world would become a better place to live in.

If all human beings contemplate on life at large and understand its purpose, meaning and intention and if each of us does his little bit to help others, then unhappiness can be wiped out of the earth. Towards the end of his career, Dreiser had come to believe that men cannot thrive by insisting on Puritanic ethics or on Darwin's theory but can thrive only if there is an atmosphere of universal love, humanism and a devotion to serve society and gain happiness by making society happy.

The present book is a revised version of my Ph.D. thesis and is an attempt to present Dreiser's "Quest for belief" and his final transformation from agnosticism to one of a believer which has not been dealt with in detail by critics. So the purpose of this investigation is to trace the development of Dreiser's belief as perceived in the course of his novels. The social background and the changing social scene have also been depicted to elucidate the impact it had on the novelist.

I wish to express my profound gratitude and indebtedness to Prof. Narayan Sharma, whose patient guidance, supervision and continuous inspiration have enabled me to carry out this work. I am grateful to the staff of American Studies Research Center/Hyderabad and United States Information Service/New Delhi for their help in providing the research material and the Vice Chancellor of Gurukul Kangri Vishwavidyalaya Professor Swatantra Kumar who has helped enable the publication of the book and for having written a valuable "Foreword" for the same. I shall remain greatly indebted to the Head of the Department of English, Professor Shrawan Kumar Sharma and his charming wife Dr. Karuna Sharma who have constantly inspired and provided the necessary encouragement and support to publish this work. My thanks are due to the University authorities for having given me the publication grant. Last but not the least I am thankful to my family who have patiently borne the long and boring evenings they had to spend on their own, thus co-operating a great deal in the course of my writing this book.

2005 Hemalatha, K.

CONTENTS

CHAPTER I

Theodore Dreiser's Intellectual Affinities and the Contemporary Literary Movements

In the last quarter of the nineteenth century, America was in a crucial phase of industrial expansion and economic development. There were abundant natural resources and it could be developed with relatively low labour and capital investment. A nation wide transportation system constructed between 1820 and 1915 also enabled Americans to exploit fully the factors of economic growth.

Merchants of each of the major Atlantic seaports - New York, Boston, Philadelphia and Baltimore promoted competitive rail road building to tap the interior Ohio Valley. The search for markets generated thousands of similar projects through- out the country . Americans in all walks of life began dreaming of economic prosperity and a successful life with new jobs, new industries, better markets and rising property values.

All this was only one side of the picture, but nevertheless they formed the impressive background in which Dreiser the pioneer of American naturalism was born in 1871. Dreiser's parents were Catholic, German speaking immigrants, and Dreiser and his brothers and sisters lived in an awful condition of poverty and misery unable to pay up their bills . Dreiser's father John Paul Dreiser was a preacher , but his mother Sarah, was loving , pious , affectionate and totally devoted to her family. Even as a young, sensitive boy, Dreiser was totally shattered to see the adverse conditions in which his family found itself. Dreiser used to weep pathetically to see his mother's torn shoes. His mother's hard work as a washerwoman in order to support the family, made the tender hearted and sympathetic, Dreiser dread poverty and long for material success.

On the one hand there were the Rockefellers and Carnegies building railroads and making a fortune out of steel and on the other hand were Dreiser and his brothers stealing coal from rail tracks to keep the hearth burning. As F.O.Mathiessen puts it : "He was a poor boy staring hungrily into the bright windows of the rich. He was himself caught for a time by the American dream of material success."[1]

Business companies were offering stocks and also forming trusts and corporations. During this period, American capitalism was gradually gaining foothold and Dreiser himself witnessed the concentration of wealth in the hands of a few. This apparent disparity where some were struggling to make both ends meet, whereas other's were wallowing in wealth and becoming stinking rich , made Dreiser desperately search an answer to the pestering question. " Is there a God ?"

Dreiser had till then believed in God being omnipotent. The question which troubled him often was : "Why then did the Devil seem so often to be in charge? Unable to reconcile his obervations with the doctrines that underlay his thinking, he was forced to see some validity in the views of his fellows, but unwilling to follow them he retained a vague faith that somehow traditional moral order would favour him in the end."[2]

Dreiser experienced a break in the puritanic moral order in his house itself. The elder children revolted against their father's orthodox beliefs and his sisters began to walk out with boys in the evenings. "In full reaction against his orthodox moralism, they were caught fast by the material unreligious aspect of things."[3]

All these reactions implicitly implied the fact that the world order was fast changing and traditional age old beliefs on morality were to be dispensed with. Class consciousness also arose quite rapidly because of the disparity between " indescribable poverty "which existed alongside "indescribable wealth ."[4]

So even as a young man Dreiser sought the world of

success and was unwilling to be shackled by his family's religious and moral beliefs. Dreiser's early reading was a mixture of Romantic and transcendental literature which include Poe, Hawthorne, Emerson, Thoreau, Laura Jean Libby and Lew Wallace. David Brion Davis observes, "At the Chicago Opera House, 'Sindbad the sailor', and 'Ali Baba And the Forty Thieves' aroused his wonder and delight."[5]

All these were childhood attractions. The main impact on his literary career was produced by naturalism and realism: movements which were already prevalent during the time. Naturalism had begun during the 1880's in France with the writer Emile Zola's book *The Naturalistic Novel.* Very few writers like Stephen Crane, and Frank Norris studied Zola. For Zola naturalism was a fictional view of life which allied itself closely to the scientific movement. Zola considered novels to be like "laboratory experiments" conducted objectively, with life supplying the novelist with plots, the novels would become reports on the novelist's finding. To an observant reporter with a keen eye for details like Dreiser, the ideas of Zola were quite appealing and he has also written his novels in the naturalistic style.

Charles Darwin's "theory of evolution" also played an important role in the forming of literary naturalists. As Hofstadter has observed in his study on the subject, "In the nineteenth and at the beginning of the twentieth century was the Darwinian century. England gave Darwin to the world, but the U.S. gave to Darwinism an unusually quick and sympathetic reception."[6]

People accepted the fact that in the struggle for survival, only the fittest would survive. Intellectuals readily accepted Darwin's principle of natural science and readily contributed to the principles of evolutionary science. Dreiser was actually influenced by an English Contemporary of Darwin, Herbert Spencer.

Herbert Spencer's book *First Principles* was read by Dreiser when he was a newspaper reporter in Pittsburgh. Spencer presented a persuasive image of man standing alone and fragile, at the mercy of immense universal forces which he could neither understand nor control. Spencer's philosophy, that " all of existence is an equilibrium of rival forces"[7] appealed to Dreiser a great deal and he himself observed bitterly, "Men lashed by storm are a bit of color in the city's life, whatever their sufferings."[8]

Reading Spencer, Dreiser wrote, had blown him "intellectually into bits"[9] by destroying the last vestiges of his belief in immutable supernaturally sanctioned moral laws .Spencer's scientific observation was that religion which dealt with the unknown was to be discarded. Space and time were equally uncertain, therefore can be dispensed with. Evolution was the unending process of change and development, where, only the fittest survive. Spencer's introductory discussions on the unknowable washed off the last vestiges of conventional religiosity in Dreiser. The supernatural, according to Spencer was "unknowable".Only the natural could be known.

Nature was a history of the evolutionary movement of all life -caused by the persistence of Force -from the simple to the complex, the unspecialized to the specialized. Within this Movement men had little significance.[10]

Man is only a part of the vast "rhythm" of life - the cosmos. Spencer also maintained in his *First Principles*[11] that the stronger man will continue to exert strength and power over the weaker and then the weaker ones will develop a self protecting power which will redress the balance which nature is never fully able to achieve. All these ideas impressed Dreiser a great deal and he has associated such ideas in his novels. If an individual is more powerful than society, at some other time society becomes more powerful than the individual and ousts him out of power. So there is a constant struggle between rival forces and constant readjustment is essential in order to maintain a balance. In an unpublished essay (1916-19) entitled "Concerning good and evil" Dreiser has observed in the Spencerian manner ,

> Something which exists originally as force or matter or both, wills to move,yet in order to do so must divide, replacing unity with variety and still maintaining a unity of sorts.There follows as a matter of course, all the elaborated phases or methods of adjustment indicated by chemistry and physics and the processes of evolution -equations of two or more movements or substances, and so - life. In order that one thing may not impinge upon another too destructively, equation is necessary.[12]

Dreiser was shaken up by all these ideas and philosophy that he became quiet a serious thinker and tried applying such thoughts in literature too . His philosophy has got encapsulated in his various novels.

Another feature of the novels of the nineteenth century was realism. Till then people had shown a preference for grotesque fables, romantic, horror tales as in Edgar Allan Poe and Hawthorne but the late nineteenth century showed a leaning towards realism. William Dean Howells, the pioneer of Realism felt that people ought to be elevated to a higher level from just browsing fables, and made to view life as a whole, to see some truth in things. People should face actual facts of life in novels. Howells was of the opinion that actual greatness comes from the facts one knows and perceives in real life. Also the author should remain aloof and not comment now and then; only then the novel will seem like real life and therefore enjoyable.

Theodore Dreiser was also influenced by Honore de Balzac, a French realist as early as 1893- 94 and August Robin who felt that there is nothing really ugly in nature or man to the artist. Art is truth and one must have the sense to scent it. Along with all these impressions of the period, Dreiser was also influenced by socialism after his visit to Russia. In his book *A Traveller at Forty* , Dreiser's sympathy at suffering humanity is quite clearly elucidated.

> I could weep just at the sight of a large,drab, hungry manufacturing town... feel sorry for ignorant humanity...

> I wish there weren't any blows, any hunger, any tears. I wish people didn't have to long bitterly for just the little thin, bare necessities... I've seen others die longing.[13]

In order to help such people who are longing to acquire things, Dreiser thought that socialism with its equal distribution of wealth would help. In actual practice Dreiser realized that the Russian slogan, "All for one and one for all" was atrocious because Dreiser was right in asking, " Can man be made to work as enthusiastically for others as for himself?.. Is not the temperament of man naturally greedy, cruel?"[14]

Dreiser was also unable to accept the idea that people could ever be made equal. He used to think that people could not be made equal in mental significance even though they could be made equal in means. "Personally, I am dubious of the result. Because I cannot even conceive of a classless society any more than I conceive of life without variations and distinctions."[15] Dreiser also felt that whether there was communism or no communism there would definitely be a difference in the mental calibre of people and also how cunning a man can be, and that would definitely make the difference. Of course Dreiser silently admired the Russian spirit of no religion, better living conditions and less amassing of wealth by individuals. Dreiser felt that : " Man's true distinction is mental,and it is a mistake to imagine that any true disfunction for man is to be derived from material possessions. There is really nothing to that."[16]

So he did not agree totally with socialism which professed that it alter the basic nature of man, also he did not approve of its interfering with human rights and privacy. Dreiser did not feel that socialism should be done away with, as D.E.S Maxwell has pointed out,

> Clearly there is a leaning towards Marxist socialism and the evolutionary theories of the formative effect of environment species. For the outright naturalist, man was the helpless plaything of impersonal economic forces, and life a struggle for existence in which only the strongest survive. This did not however, prevent his

> believing that humanity might somehow rise against these forces and direct them to more beneficient needs.[17]

Dreiser believed that incidents should be reported as the writer saw them, and his own experience provided him with ample information. If he had allowed his characters to transgress moral codes of conduct then that was because of his belief in man's instinctive and impulsive reactions to incidents. Dreiser has termed impulsive actions as chemisms. In his enthusiasm to record beautiful incidents he has not left out the ugly, unimpressive and derogatory social and moral codes of behaviour. Dreiser told an interviewer in 1907,

> Every human being is intensely interesting. If the human being has ideals, the struggle and the attempt to realize those ideals, the going back on his own trail, the failure, the success, the reason for the individual failure, the individual success -all these things are interesting, interesting even when there are no ideals, where there is only the personal desire to survive, the fight to win, the stretching out of the fingers to grasp - these are the things I want to write about.[18]

While being influenced by Darwin's biological determinism or "Survival of Fittest," Dreiser was also aware that social determinism would eventually win. Societies which happen to be stronger would definitely crush the weaker ones and emerge successful. What remains is beauty and eternal goodness.

> What we plainly see is birth and deaththe result of chemic and electro physical processes of which at bottom we know exactly nothing. And beyond that murder, the chase, life living on life, the individual sustaining himself at the expense of every other, and wishing not to die. And then beauty, beauty, beauty, which seems to derive as much and more from this internecine and wholly heartless struggle as from any other thing. And yet beauty, beauty, beauty - the entire process, to the human eye at least,

aesthetic in its results if by no means entirely so in its processes.[19]

Here we find that in some respects Dreiser resembles the romantics like Wordsworth or Keats. As Donald Pfizer writes : "Dreiser's characters like Wordsworth's, also "half perceive" and "half create." But because of the focus of their vision is a cityscape rather than a landscape, the stream, field, tree and flower of the poet become, in Dreiser's fiction a street, a theatre, hotel, mansion. Nevertheless Dreiser's world still has the resources of romantic iconography."[20]

Such beauty then can transform the whole world into something which is lovable and which needs to be worshipped. The study of Dreiser's novels and poems reveal not only, naturalism, realism, determinism or Darwinism but something more deeper and thought provoking than that. With complete abandon he has allowed himself to be engulfed by his experiences. Dreiser is like a man groping in the dark trying to understand the basic scheme of things. There is a soul searching to understand the mystery of this world.

After all the scientific inquiry into this world, Dreiser felt that science would have to admit defeat with regard to questions relating to the ultimate fountain of all creations. "For all its knowledge of how, science cannot say Why."[21] This mystery of the creative force seized his mind and in his later years he began taking down notes on God and religion.Once again Dreiser began giving a spiritual and religious interpretation of the creative force.

Dreiser conceived of God as the force which controls the cosmos and of which each living being is an atom or a part.

> The totality of all its forms and their ramifications -is no more than a fragment or special and yet minute extension of a much greater life- the Supreme directive forces of the universe which creates , regulates and qualifies all that by man is called human life, or animal or vegetable

life.[22]

Also venturing in the same strain he adds in his *Introduction to Thoreau* (P.2) that this directive force can be known by various nomenclatures as "Spirit", "Brahma", "Divine Essence" or "Force". There is a transitional growth in Dreiser as we see him in his books and poems. As a young man he was analysing the mystery of the world without grasping any meaning but ultimately the meaning seemed to become clearer and clearer that life is a totality of experiences; each man is a part of a whole or cosmos and that one can see himself in another creation of the Supreme Power.

Dreiser who began with,
My faith was nothing
An illusion
And that life is nothing
An illusion.[23]

grew, matured and with full of love for all God's creations he was later able to exclaim,

Great is shimtu, the Adder God,
. . . .
. . . .
Shimtu, the Adder My God.[24]

His all encompassing love reached a climax when he readily accepted an Adder as his God .

In his novels also this growth in logic is visible. In the earlier novels, *Sister Carrie* and *Jennie Gerhardt* there is a search for a theory of existence. *The Financier, Titan and The Stoic* deals with materialistic success which is linked with his own period of monetary success in life. A sense of Beauty is revealed in *Genius. The American Tragedy* deals with social and biological determinisms with the belief in progress as a result of change in the environment and the acceptance of the fact that man can become better by his own will and efforts. But it is in *The Stoic* and in *The Bulwark* that his growth is complete and Dreiser experiences a sense of beauty and universal love in all living things.

In *The Bulwark* Dreiser has recorded an experience of how once he came across a puff adder and thinking that it would be poisonous killed it. Later on he understood that it was a mistake and the next time he saw an adder he spoke to it. The snake seemed to have understood his speech, and it quietly went away. This incident made him understand the harmony between all of God's creations. Thus the Quest for faith in Dreiser grew by degrees and attained a full some growth in his understanding of love which reigns supreme in all God's creation.

Dreiser did not believe in institutionalized religion, singing psalms or in performing of ceremonies but believed in something beyond it which could liberate human beings, thereby enlightening them with an elevated and more magnanimous and accommodating soul which could perceive a universal bonding. In his "Confession of Faith" Dreiser has declared : "I believe in the compelling power of love .I do not understand it. I believe it to be the most fragrant blossom of all this theory of existence."[25]

Theodore Dreiser's main purpose of writing was to make America rise up intellectually, spiritually and economically.

> We, more than any nation, because ours was the youth and the strength, were to lift and maintain aloft the banner of intellectual and spiritual freedom. We were to do tremendous things, not for the human pocketbook but the human mind and soul.Our children and our children's children were to be free, progressive,fearless, mentally and spiritually alert loosened from the trammels and chains of superstition and the degradation of poverty and want[26]

In this purpose Dreiser resembled the Romantics whose main intention was also the same. They also wished that the "repressed energy of love and goodness -his (man's) essential nature,"[27] should come to the fore front and not be allowed to be suppressed by the state. Dreiser firmly believed that only the capacity which is inherent in a man at birth itself can be tapped and nothing new can be made of a human being. "What life does is to develop and train especial inherent capacities. . . but the instinct, and the ability to foreknow to appreciate, understand, these things are not taught in schools."[28]

The fact that man is only a "waif" or "accident" in Nature always troubled Dreiser. Man found himself struggling to make his own "pathetic way in the world."[29] But this should not prevent him from hard work and lead him into a lethargic acceptance of life as it were. Therefore Dreiser felt that man should be like Prometheus fighting until the last even though he knew that he was only a "minute tool in the hands of something more significant than himself"[30]

> I, for one, think so, and, for my part would prefer to be a seeking Prometheus chained to a rock and my liver gnawed daily by an eagle of an irritated and Jealous higher power than a crawling worm or whimpering slave praying for some endless Nirvana . . . [31]

Dreiser who began with skepticism in the beginning of life questioning God's designs ultimately came to accept him as the master designer who, " Far from being blind was the cause of order and pattern in the cosmos."[32] It was with this realization that he read Hindu philosophy from the Gita and gained a lot of knowledge that calmed down his puzzled mind. In "The Stoic"we find such quotations as: "No human being can give up action altogether, but he who gives up the fruits of action is said to be non attached.[33] Dreiser and his wife Helen visited the ' Vedanta Center'[34] in Los Angeles and got their ideas on Vedanta clarified.

Dreiser's social concern and the belief in a creator who could create an ordered cosmos out of chaos are implicit in his writings. A hater of war and chaos, lover of mystery and wonder of life Dreiser strongly advocated universal love as the panacea for all ills in society. "If you wish a loving and helpful God to exist and to have mercy, be Him. There is no other way." This statement exemplifies in a nutshell the realization which dawned upon him on his final and crucial phase of his " Quest For Belief."

NOTES AND REFERENCES

[1]F.O. Mathiessen , *Theodore Dreiser* (New York: Dell Publishing Co., (1966) 4.

[2]RobertH.Elias, *Theodore Dreiser :Apostle Of Nature* (NewYork:Alfred A. Knopf Inc.,1949) 40.

[3]Mathiessen, *Theodore Dreiser* 6.

[4]Theodore Dreiser. *A Book About Myself* (New York:Boni and Liveright,1922) 459.

[5]David Brion David, *Dreiser and Naturalism Revisited: The Stature of Theodore Dreiser.* Ed.Alfred Kazin and Charles Shapiro.(Bloomington:Indiana University Press, 1965) 231.

[6]Richard Hofstadter, *Social Darwinism In American Thought* Rev. Ed. (Boston, 1965) 4-5.

[7]Elias, *Theodore Dreiser: Apostle of Nature* 50.

[8]Elias, *Theodore Dreiser: Apostle of Nature* 50.

[9] Dreiser, *A Book About Myself* 97.

[10]Donald Pfizer , *The Novels of Theodore Dreiser* (Minneapolis: Univ. of Minnesota Press ,1976) 10.

[11]Herbert Spencer, "Rhythm of motion" *FirstPrinciples* (New York, 1886) 250-271.

[12]Pfizer, *The Novels of Theodore Dreiser* 11.

[13] Dreiser, *A Traveller at Forty*, (New York: Century,1923) 43.

[14] Dreiser, *Dreiser looks at Russia* (New York,1928) 77.

[15] Dreiser, *Dreiser looks at Russia*, 79.

[16] Dreiser, Dreiser looks at Russia, 245.

[17]D.E.S. Maxwell, *American Fiction : The Intellectual Background* (London: Routledge & Kegan Paul,1963) 294.

[18]Otis Norman, "Talk with Four Novelists" New York Times Saturday Review of Books,(June 15,1907) 393.

[19]Dreiser,"What I believe,"*The Forum,*LXXXII {Nov. 1929} 80.

[20]Pfizer, *The Novels of Theodore Dreiser* 21.

[21]Dreiser, *Theodore Dreiser presents the living thoughts of Thoreau* (New York:Longmans, Green.& Co., 1946) 2.

[22]Dreiser, "The Myth of Reality" Typescript N.D (U.P.)

[23]Dreiser ,*Hidden God* , Selected Poems From Moods By Robert Palmer Saalbach (New York: Exposition Press, 1969) 67.

[24]Dreiser, *Hidden God,* 142.

[25]Dreiser, " Confession of Faith " N. D. (Written at 3609 Broadway, New York),U.P.

[26]Dreiser, *Hey Rub-A-Dub-Dub*, 25.

[27]Milton R. Stern, "American values and Romantic Fiction" From *American Classics Revisited* Ed. P. C. Kar and D. Ramakrishna (Hyderabad: ASRC , 1985) 55.

[28]Milton R. Stern, 123.

[29]Dreiser, *Hey Rub-A-Dub-Dub*, 123.

[30]Dreiser, *Hey Rub-A-Dub-Dub*, 116.

[31]Dreiser, *Hey Rub-A-Dub-Dub*, 125.

[32]R.N.Mookerjee, Theodore Dreiser. "His thought and Social Criticism" (Delhi: National Publishers, 1974) 203.

[33]Dreiser, *The Stoic* (New York: Doubleday,1947), 291.

[34]Marguerite Tjader, *Dreiser. A New Dimension* (Connecticut:Silvermine Publishers,1965) 239-241.

[35] Dreiser, *The Hidden God* Typescript N.D "U.P"

CHAPTER II

Sister Carrie and Jennie Gerhardt: Search For a theory of existence

As a young man, Dreiser himself had been struggling in the grips of poverty. He had always been watching with envy young men, wearing silk shirts and protecting their hands with gloves. The disparity between aristocracy and lower middle class people had always been a source of depression and hatred to Dreiser. Those who were struggling hard to make both ends meet, appear to be quite vulnerable and appear as if they were mere puppets in the hands of fate.

The condition of the American system longing for material success is clearly elaborated by Dreiser in his *The Color of a Great City.*

> Unfortunately the money problem, once solved, is not the only thing in the world. Their lives, although they reach the place where they have gold signs, automobiles and considerable private pleasures are none the more beautiful. Too often, because of these early conditions, they remain warped, oppressive, greedy and distorted in every worthy mental sense by the great fight they have made to get their money. Nearly the only ideal that is set before these strugglers...is the one of getting money. A hundred thousand children are innoculated in infancy with the doctrine that wealth is all the shabbiest and most degrading doctrine that can be impressed upon anyone.[1]

Sister Carrie is Dreiser's first novel and it depicts Dreiser as a realist, in the last quarter of the nineteenth century. In this novel Dreiser presents the transit of America to urbanisation and industrialisation and the resultant drop in moral values and ethics.

The novel *Sister Carrie* is based on the story of his sister Emma who had eloped with a much older person Hopkins in 1886. The story is about a young attractive girl Carrie Meeber, who, wishing to succeed in life, boards the train to Chicago in Columbia City, Wisconsin in 1889. She is "full of the illusions of ignorance and youth."[2] As is usual in such a case she is drawn towards Charles Drouet a flashy young gentleman with a wallet full of flashy greenbacks.As for Carrie her understanding of the moral significance of money was the popular understanding, nothing more. "The old definition:'Money,something everybody else has and I must get,' would have expressed her understanding of it thoroughly."[3]

At the very beginning of the novel it is evident that Carrie is looking for methods by which to improve her lot in society. She would get in one of the great shops and do some kind of job until she gets rewarded or until something happened. She did not know exactly what she wanted .She did not think of marrying Drouet either. Dreiser adds that "Things would go on, though, in a dim kind of way until the better thing would eventuate, and Carrie would be rewarded for toiling in the city."4

This is the opinion she gets when she steps on to the first step of the ladder of success with Drouet offering her two soft, green ten dollar bills to get herself new clothes. The presence of money and the urge to buy new clothes forces her to leave the security of her sister Minnie's house and venture out alone into the world of money. The twenty dollar in her hand seems a wonderful thing. She feels that plenty of money would clear away all troubles. In a sense, it appears as if Carrie had sold herself for a suit of clothes.

Securing a job for oneself, not being as simple as Carrie imagines it to be, Carrie encounters a hopeless situation of not being able to find a job. Once again Prince Charming, Charles Drouet meets her and assists her in fending for herself at Chicago.He took her about a great deal, spent money upon her, and when he travelled took her with him.It is then that she gets introduced to

Hurstwood the manager of Fitzerald and Moy's .Carrie sees that Hurstwood is a man who is "more clever than Drouet in a hundred ways."[5]

Subsequently with a strong will and passion for ascending in life Carrie takes to role playing. The lure of the theatre with its glamour, tension, applause, fine clothes, and so on is quite tempting and she is drawn towards it. She has a vivid imagination and verve to do things.

> She saw herself in a score of pathetic situations in which she assumed a tremulous voice and suffering manner. Her mind delighted itself with scenes of luxury and refinement, situations in which she was the cynosure of all eyes, the arbiter of all fates. ..[6]

Admired and advised by Drouet as to how to dress up in order to augment her charm, she arrives closer to Hurstwood. Carrie with her sharp eye for detail has the power to grasp and rise up to become the beloved of Hurstwood, the intelligent, affluent gentleman with a powerful voice .

It is surprising to find that Carrie compares the clothes of Hurstwood and Drouet, and naturally Drouet who had actually taught Carrie finesse is now beheld far short of Hurstwood as far as his own clothes are concerned.Carrie has risen so much in luxury that she is able to clearly perceive the difference. Hurstwood is irresistibly tempted to elope with Carrie and is ruined in the process. While he is alone, closing Hannah and Hogg's for the night, he is tempted by the $10,000 that he has in the locker in front of him.

> The wavering of a mind under such circumstances is an almost inexplicable thing, and yet it is absolutely true....He was drawn by such a keen desire for Carrie, driven by such a state of turmoil in his own affairs that he thought constantly it would be best, and yet he wavered.[7]

The flaw in Hurstwood's character becomes a tragic flaw which ruins him. Excessive lust for money can never bring fruitful rewards. Unfortunately while he tries to resist the temptation and put back the money, fate intervenes and he finds that the locker has got locked by accident. Afraid of what might be in store for him - loss of family, property and position he elopes with Carrie Meeber to New York.

This only brings about the steady rise of Carrie and the subsequent decline of Hurstwood.Hurstwood invests the bulk of his capital in a saloon partnership but the building in which he holds his lease is sold to make room for a newedifice. His capital sinks, he finds no employment and becomes untidy, lazy and shabbily dressed. In the following passage Dreiser points out how some men are unaware of the turn in fortune until such time they are at a total loss and fortune is wrested from them.

> Fortune like a man is as organism ... It may be conserved by the growth of a community or of a state,it may be involved in providing something for which there is a growing demand. This removes it at once beyond the special care of the founder. It needs not so much foresight now as direction. The man wanes, the need continues or grows and fortune , fallen into whose hands it may, continues. Hence some men never recognise the turning in the tide of their abilities.[8]

Once again it is Carrie who controls the situation; she once again gets a very inconspicuous place in a musical comedy but soon is able to establish herself as the breadwinner. Finding herself unable to support Hurstwood for long she leaves behind a note that she could not support and pay the rent and that she was leaving him forever. Twenty dollars she left behind for his use and added, " You can do whatever you like with the furniture. I don't want it."[9]

This selfish, rather ruthless behaviour leads to the end of Hurstwood and the eventual rise of Carrie to a comfortable position with : "her purse bursting with good green bills of comfortable denominations . . . . She could look about on her gowns again."[10] Drouet tries to enter her life but is dismissed, another actor Bob

Ames who attempts to get her straight dramatic roles is the man in her life now. She should reach higher and higher in order to reach her final happiness. There is thus a constant struggle for social ascendancy;a struggle against all odds to rise in society. There seem to be no qualms of conscience, just the basic animal desire for male companions and they are also discarded when found to be no longer useful.

In *Sister Carrie* we find that the characters Carrie, Drouet, Hurstwood and others are at the mercy of incomprehensible forces within and without over which man has no control. In Carrie there is an internal drive that sways and controls all her passions and emotions and urges her to move forward. In the presence of such all consuming drive to achieve, morals and ethics seem to be out of question, they have no place in society. "Dreiser employs the rocking chair to symbolize the restlessness and feverish activity that transport Carrie to no satisfying destination."[11]

She is driven by an urge to hope for ultimate and everlasting joy; she symbolises the typical American urge to long for material success. Unfortunately monetary success is so deceptive that the more one has, the more one longs to have, and the search is endless. We leave Carrie at a point when she is not very happy and feels that perhaps her fate is "forever to be the pursuit of that radiance of delight which tints the distant hilltops of the world." Thus at the end of the novel, Carrie is "enticed into the quick sands of materialism by those mirages of success that hangs so alluringly in amethyst skies."[11] Dreiser closes the novel addressing Carrie thus : "Know, then, that for you is neither surfeit nor content. In your rocking chair, by your window dreaming, shall you dream such happiness as you may never feel."[12] The inevitable frustration that goes with such a horrific pursuit of wealth is explicitly elucidated by this observation.

Not only *Sister Carrie* but also Dreiser's *Jennie Gerhardt* are examples of the typical American women struggling to rise above poverty and ascend socially. This social ascendancy is as evasive as a mirage and the more one tries to grasp it the more it recedes. *Jennie Gerhardt* is another novel of Dreiser's which depicts how the social and economic condition of man shapes his life. *Jennie Gerhardt* is autobiographical in the sense that it reveals Dreiser's own condition and his family when he was young. Dreiser's father was religious and believed totally in God but did nothing more concrete than that in maintaining his family. Dreiser's mother was quite a resourceful, hardworking, gentle and pragmatic woman who did her best to run the family. In *Jennie Gerhardt* also we find Mrs. Gerhardt scrubbing floors at times and washing linen at other times to make both ends meet.

The reference to Gerhardt's children picking coal from cars on the eve of Christmas was a dire poignant reality true to Dreiser's boyhood too. The result of such a condition is quite natural with Senator Brander enamoured by the beauty and pathetic condition of Jennie helping out the family with knicknacks - a Christmas tree, toys and groceries.

Pity turns to love when Jennie turned to Senator Brander for help in releasing her brother Sebastian from prison for having stolen coal, he helps her out, but their relationship turn out to be intimate and it is quite unfortunate that Jennie becomes pregnant. Senator Brander plans to marry her but dies subsequently due to typhoid.

Unlike *Sister Carrie* where blind chance operates quite often, like the chance meeting with Drouet and Hurstwood, the automatic locking of the bank locker and so on, in *Jennie Gerhardt* we find that even though chance operates as in the sudden death of Senator Brander , Dreiser is more convinced and convincing ,that man is less a victim of chance or external forces. Man suffers because of his own doings; of his own incapacity to decide an act. The pressures of life are so many that man gropes in the dark unable to decide and accept that which is soul - satisfying and morally binding.

In *Jennie Gerhardt* the conflict is between materialism and spiritualism. Money is the main attraction in the early part of the novel . The attraction of Jennie towards Senator Brander a tall, straight shouldered, imposing and opulent man , is money. "Poverty and beauty certainly made up an affecting combination,"[13] is Dreiser's observation of the situation. As for Jennie Gerhardt, "There lay deep seated in her conscious deprecation of poverty and shame of having to own any need."[14]

In *Jennie Gerhardt* we find that Jennie's father Mr. William Gerhardt is a devout religionist and when Jennie's child is born, it is he who insisted on getting a priest to baptize the child. "Religion was not a thing of mere words or interesting ideas to be listened to on Sunday but a strong, vital expression of the Divine Will handed down from a time when men were in personal contact with God."[15]

Despite the struggle for existence and while the family attempts to fight poverty, Old Gerhardt's main concern is to follow precepts of religion very sincerely and work to enrich the baby's soul with knowledge of God. Lester Kane is the opposite of Gerhardt. He is a typical representative of the age and society of the late nineteenth, early twentieth century America. With no belief in religion or sanctity of marriage, he is, brought up as the heir to a comfortable fortune and it was expected that he would marry in his own sphere, but Lester Kane was not sure he wanted to get married at all."Of course the conjugal state was an institution...The whole nation believed in it.True but other nations believed in polygamy."[16]

Lester Kane seems to depict Dreiser's own views whereas Gerhardt's behaviour is like Dreiser's father's. Whatever else could one expect from an age of the railroad ,the post office, the telephone, the telegraph, the newspaper, and a host of other material advancements, when money and not morals was the chief concern of a vast majority of the population . "Lester Kane was the natural product of these untoward conditions."[17]

This sort of atmosphere is the cause of insomnia in some and madness in others. Mechanization, industry and a fast pace of life have all interrupted the normal smooth and balanced working of the human mind and men are not able to cope with intensive advancement in almost all spheres of human activity .Even brothers, Lester and Robert, though outwardly friendly, are poles apart in business matters.

While Lester was for building up trade through friendly relationship, concessions, personal contact and favours, Robert was for pulling everything tight,cutting down the cost of production, and offering such "financial inducements as would throttle competition."[18]

In such a demanding world where money is considered to be the be-all and end-all of life, Jennie wishes to wipe out poverty and she wishes to hide the shameful condition of herself and her family. This makes Jennie fall down a step further and mother a child. It is quite surprising to find that the brother for whom she has made such a great sacrifice has more clear cut views of life. Sebastian, her brother is quite practical regarding the road to success: "To succeed one must do something - one must associate or atleast seem to associate, with those who were foremost in the world of appearances... clothes were the main touchstone. If men wore nice clothes and had rings and pins,whatever they did seemed appropriate."[19]

Sebastian works in a cigar store in Cleveland. The family, consisting of mother and younger children join him there, and struggle to make a comfortable living. It is then that the young mother Jennie who works as a maid in the wealthy Bracebridges, is met by a guest Lester Kane, an opulent young gentleman and is accepted by him as his mistress.

Lester Kane is handsome, has a magnetic charm about him which draws her in but the main factor which brings about the liaison is poverty. Ironically her explanation to Lester Kane for her surrender to Brander is, "We were so terribly poor."[20]Dreiser has observed how poverty made it essential for her to go with him in the beginning: "He had only to say, "come" and she must obey, it was her destiny."[21] Unfortunately even though Lester loves her well enough to take care of her he is unable to , " legalise her anomalous position and to face the world bravely with the fact that he had chosen a wife who suited him. .."[22]

The unfair situation in which Jennie finds herself is quite depressing and Dreiser is unable to digest the predicament in which his famous heroine finds herself in. Lester has a spiritual affinity with her but still cannot accept her as his wife. No, he cannot do that because she has been working as a lady's maid, moreover she has a daughter Vesta - an illegal daughter as a result of her illegal relationship with Senator Brander. All this prevents Lester from perfecting their relationship through the bond of marriage. Socially she is not suited to him. As Dreiser himself comments: "He (Lester) did care for her in an elemental way, but he was hedged about by the ideas of the conventional world in which he had been reared."[23]

So unfortunately even though there was a spiritual bondage between the two their love needs to be thwarted. Moreover on revelation of the fact that Jennie is already the mother of a child through Senator Brander, "Lester reveals himself as a man powerfully conditioned by the assumptions of his class and sex despite his conception of himself as a New Man."[24]

Here Lester behaves as if he is a criminal court judge and treats Jennie as if she is a criminal standing before him asking for justice. "Jennie was before him as the criminal at the bar. He, the righteous, the moral, the pure of heart, was in the judgement seat.Now to sentence her - to make up his mind what course of action he should pursue."[25] Even though he feels like leaving her, the comforts to which he has got used to, prevent him from doing so, and so he decides to leave the matter for the present and may be not marry her at all, but continue to live with her. This attitude is not at all surprising because Lester was an aristocrat and he could decide on the fate of those who served him.

There is a difference between Sister Carrie's attraction to

Drouet and Jennie's attraction to Kane. Carrie accepts Drouet as a stepping stone in her ladder of success where as Jennie's attraction is more sublime and less self centered. Hers is a selfless sacrifice and spiritual bondage which though not deeply understood by Lester in the beginning is later on acknowledged by him as a " spiritual affinity ." " Not only because he was in Chicago but because he had never been spiritually separated from Jennie. He was thinking about her constantly at this time."[26]

Jennie actually learns social manners and etiquettes and perfects herself to his taste. She is "true and good and womanly to the very centre of her being,"[27] and Lester totally depends on her for his creature comforts. Despite all this Jennie faces social injustice because of poverty. Lester's explanation to her depicts the inability of humans to have control over their fate : "All of us are more or less Pawns. We are moved about like chessmen by circumstances over which we have no control,"[28] is unsatisfactory and he could have easily sacrificed his wealth of about a million and a half for just ten thousand a year but he does not. So Jennie's love seems to be on a higher plane than Carrie's , Jennie is more stoic, passionate and devoted to her lover.

Lester himself feels that she is indispensable and he could not desert her. Her poverty, devotion and her spiritual compatibility with Lester makes her feel totally distraught to see him in his deathbed. She looks back and reminiscences on all his good deeds - 0f how he took care of her family in Cleveland and of his "generous treatment of Gerhardt, and all the long ago tokens of love and kindness."[29]

Carrie, on the other hand, only wishes for social ascendancy and is unconcerned about Drouet or Hurstwood's death even. So Carrie's social ascendancy seems to be a mirage whereas Jennie ascends morally and spiritually. Even when Letty, a lady of high society marries Lester, Jennie brings up Vesta and lives alone and when Vesta dies of typhoid, Jennie brings up two more orphans. Morally, spiritually and emotionally she feels that she belongs to Lester only and none else than Lester. This devotion is absent in

Sister Carrie.

Jennie Gerhardt, is a glass blower's daughter with six brothers and sisters to take care of, when her father burnt his hands at the glass works and is jobless. So naturally she needs substantial moral and financial support. According to Lester himself, only that man can make a success of life who has poverty to spur him to success .

As a rule a man needs poverty to help him to his enthusiasm, and youth. The thing he has discovered, and with which he is going to busy himself, must be the door to a thousand opportunities and a thousand joys. Happiness must be beyond or the fire will not burn as brightly as it might - the urge will not be great enough to make a success.[30]

Lester's philosophy is true of Jennie who has spiritual growth in her character having remained loyally devoted to the wealthy son of an industrialist. The persistence and unfaltering nature of her of her love of him until and even after death did part them is remarkable. Dreiser's observation, "Did anything matter except goodness - goodness of heart? What else was there that was real?"[31] is elucidative of the fact that even though the society does not value goodness, goodness of heart is the most precious jewel a human being can have. From both these novels it is implicit that Dreiser understood the great motivating force for American society - it was money -they were materialistic to the core. Philip Gerber observes:

> The money ideal would be exposed as the great motivating purpose of life in the United States where one's affluence determined the degree of creature comfort one might enjoy, the measure of prestige one might claim, the extent of social power one might command... Individuals claw their way upward, consuming conspicuously along the trail, rising by means fair or foul. One summit is reached only to reveal another, loftier, more magnetic in appeal...[32]

Alongside the treatment of rise and success in one's career there was also another favourite theme of Dreiser's - one of living together for convenience's sake without tying the nuptial knot. "He would not wear the social shackles if it were possible to satisfy the needs of his heart and nature and still remain free and unfettered.[33]

This theme is repeated once and again in *Sister Carrie,* in Roberta and Clyde's relationship in *American Tragedy* and so on. Also the theme of struggle for existence is exaggerated by the fact that the heroine goes from shop to shop in search 0f a job, and finds none. This is what makes the condition more and more pathetic. In Jennie Gerhardt we find that: " Wherever she went, no one seemed to want any help. She applied at the stores, the factories, the little shops that lined the outlying thorough fares, but was always met by a rebuff ." [34]

The condition of Sister Carrie when out on a job hunting errand , is none the better. After having tried her luck at several shops, departmental stores and being refused a job, "When she had gotten safely into the street she could scarcely restrain her tears."[35] Having spent a whole day looking for job and being rejected ,she was miserable and dejected at "her own helplessness without quite realising the wisp on the tide that she was."[36]

It only shows how insignificant the individual is in front of a materialistic and capitalistic society. She feels totally helpless and unnoticed by any munificent, magnanimous shop keeper. Sister Carrie's condition is quite pathetic and unfair too, because the moneyed class or aristocrats and businessman are making more and more money, wearing bright, shiny clothes and are unfamiliar with the meaning of "poverty" whereas those on the other side of the scale are unfairly crushed and trampled upon by society.

Sister Carrie did not have any hard and fast opinion as far as morals or principles are concerned. Therefore she is ready to drift away quite easily without any pricking of her conscience. All that which is foremost in her brain is to secure a position for herself in society. "there was no household law to govern her" [37]

Minnie her sister also has a premonition of Sister Carrie's fate. Minnie dreams that her sister is drifting and sinking into a pit, unable to draw herself up, until she is ultimately engulfed by the water down below. "She seemed to rescue, and now it was difficult to call her."[38] This mysterious dream is quite meaningful as far as Carrie is concerned for it predicts the fact that in her search for a way to escape poverty, she is slowly drifting away from her sister and is soon to find herself in an irredeemable position and her sister could do nothing to save her.

The unprincipled pursual of money has its parallel in *Hey Rub- A-Dub-Dub* also in the following passage which very clearly describes how the American society was blindly pursuing money without any moral pricking of any kind,

> The fierce, rudimentary mass mind ofAmerica like that of some inchoate,Primeval monster, relentlessly concentrated in the appetite of the moment, knows nothing as yet apparently of its own vast,inert almost nerveless body encrusted with parasites. One looks out today over the immense vista of our society, stretching westward in a succession of dreary steppes, and one realises what it means to possess no cultural initiative or tradition, filling in the interstices of energy and maintaining a steady current of life over and above the ebb and flow of individual necessity or animal appetite or purpose. Money, money, money.[39]

Dreiser gives very elaborate description of the clothes worn by different characters. Describing Hurstwood's clothes Dreiser observes:

> His clothes were particularly new and rich in appearance. The coat lapels stood out with that medium stiffness which excellent, cloth possesses.The vest was of a rich Scotch plaid,set with a double row of round mother-of- buttons. His cravate was a shiny combination of silken threads.[40]

and so on. As for Carrie herself her interest is in those aspects of life in which she would be admired by one and all. "Her mind delighted itself with scenes of luxury and refinement, situation in which she was the cynosure of all eyes, the arbiter of all fates."[41] Carrie is not totally without guidance either; Ames a friend of her has told her "that riches were not everything; there was a great deal more in the world than she knew; that the stage was good, and the literature she read poor." [42]

The fact to be perceived that while some are stinking rich, there are others who are miserable and live in slums. If Carrie were to remember them and adjust herself to her situation than there would have been no problem whatsoever. It is because she has dreams of acquisition and quite ready to offer herself for the acquisition of more wealth that she is ruined. As Dreiser has himself pointed the lure is quite gnawing and difficult to overcome. "Aye! dreams unfulfilled gnawing, luring, idle phantoms which beckon and lead... until death and dissolution dissolve their power and restore us blind to nature's heart. [43]

This passage has elucidated the fact that riches would definitely be followed by dissolution and death and there is no escape from this aftermath of accumulation of wealth. If only Carrie, Drouet or Hurtswood could understand it, then they would have definitely been saved and not ruined.

The fact is that the society had dropped so much into the myth of financial success that the idealist or dreamer who was interested in admiring Nature was looked down upon by the ones who were crazily absorbed in accumulation of wealth. The following passage from *Jennie Gerhardt* is indicative of this fact.

> That other world of flesh into which has been woven pride and greed looks askance at the idealist, the dreamer. If one says it is sweet to look at the clouds, the answer is a warning against idealness. If one seeks to give ear to the winds, it shall be well with his soul but they will seize upon his possessions.[44]

So what ever one does to get close to nature, to what is real, ideal, the society is not going to allow one to go near it; it will have its brakes and it would divert them for what is real, Absolute to that which is fleeting and for the time being only -MONEY.

When one plans to get more and more money, a single thing whether it is a razor or a soap, it obsesses the mind so much that one cannot but make profit from it. Describing the character of Lester in *Jennie Gerhardt* , Dreiser has pointed out this fact that Lester Kane is unfortunately or fortunately not such a ruthless business man."It means that one thing, a cake of soap, a new can-opener, a safety razor or speed accelerator, must seize on your imagination with tremendous force,burn as a raging flame,and make itself the be-all and end-all of your existence. [45]

Dreiser had himself felt while he was young, that he too should join in the money hunt but later on he decided against it for he felt that he did not have "the kind of ability"[46] which is needed to make the money with and it seemed to him as if he was being questioned by the city " why so incompetent? why so idle? so poor? Why live in such a wretched neighbourhood? Why not cross over and join the great gay throng, make a successful way for yourself? Why sit aside from this great game of materiality and pretend to ignore it or to feel superior?"[47]

The cities were thus a great attraction for all those aspiring to make fast buck. Even though Dreiser himself was attracted, as shown by the above passage, he some how resisted, but characters like Sister Carrie, Drouet, Lester Kane are all trapped by the aspiration to become richer, at sometime or the other in their lives.Lester Kane of Jennie Gerhardt is a man who did not wish to be trapped by the convention of society. But it becomes impossible as he is unable to actually do so. His father's will offering him legacy only if he married an aristocratic woman leaves him with no choice but to return to a conventional form of life. So it is clear that even if an individual wishes to break away from conventions, society would not allow it to happen.

Jennie Gerhardt's character reminds one of Hardy's *Tess of D'urbervilles* who is proclaimed by Hardy to be a "Pure Woman". Here also in *Jennie Gerhardt*, Jennie is a victim of circumstances which get together to ruin her. What Dreiser wishes us to understand is that she has an essentially pure spirit:- "The spirit of Jennie-Who shall express it? This daughter of poverty. ..was a creature of mellowness of temperament which words can but vaguely suggest." [48]

Jennie, even though she needs material as well as spiritual support from Lester, is ready to leave him so that he would become a more prosperous man. Unfortunately such a noble soul is looked down upon by the so called elite or aristocratic society. They do not care for her sensitivity or spiritual affinity with Lester. All that his sister or family members are bothered about is how to preserve the honour of the family. As she is a washer woman's daughter she could not be included as a member of their family. So when given a cold shoulder by Lester's sister Louise, Jennie observes: "So this was her real position in another woman's eyes. Now she could see what the world thought. This family was as aloof from her as if it lived on another planet. To his sisters and brothers, his father and mother, she was a bad woman, a creature far beneath him socially, far beneath him mentally and morally, a creature of the streets.[49]

The readers as well as Lester feel that Jennie is not " a creature of the streets" According to Lester's own estimate: "She's a good housekeeper. She's an ideal mother .She's the most affectionate creature under the sun."[50] To both Lester and Jennie this is the true state of affairs that they can not escape the judgement to be passed by society. "When men or women err-that is pass out from the sphere in which they are accustomed to move...so well defined is the sphere of social activity that he who departs from it is doomed."[51]

Dreiser has himself observed in the essay , "Neurotic America and the Sex Impulse" that such moral or physical constraints in the name of religion or class would oppose the individual's biologic necessity and the chances are that he would go crazy .Jennie-Lester relationship has also had such a lot of resistance from society that it is difficult to estimate the level of ruin it had caused Lester.

> The physical laws which seem to govern the biologic impulse after it expresses itself in the shape of youth, or man, and compels it for purposes of social expression to submit to restraints and equation . . .But this does not provide us with exact rules for conducting ourselves here or how best to subdue or balance with other things,the enormous fires with which we sometimes find ourselves lit.[52]

Dreiser has pointed out that moreover all such social restrictions are a matter of convenience and nothing more. Each nation, each civilization has its own set of codes each entirely different from the other. Jennie has accompanied Lester in his world wide tours and has understood that morals are dependent on climate, religious beliefs and so on and that nothing is fixed.

> She learned of an older civilization,powerful, complex, complete. Millions of people had lived and died here, believing other conditions of existence... their differences in standards of morals were due sometimes to climate, sometimes to religious oeliefs, and sometimes to the rise of peculiar personalities like Mohammed.[53]

Thus there could never be a set code of morals or any hard and fast rule regarding morality. Jennie's fall is because society does not wish her to rise and make amends in society, for her earlier lapse. Society had not identified her presence; wealth and position work as barriers to separate her Lester. So, for Jennie Gerhardt who struggles hard to rise high in society, all that she is left with after Lcster's death are the two orphan children whom she adopts. Somehow Jennie has come to understand that peace of mind can be attained only by helping others to come up in life. She devotes her time and attention to the two needy children, but once again when they would grow up and get married, she would be left alone.

Even Lester is able to form a critical view of life, after the death of Jennie's daughter Vesta:

> In distant ages a queer thing had come to pass. There had started on its way in the form of evolution a minute cellular organism which had reproduced itself by division, had early learned to combine itself with others, to organize itself into bodies, strange forms of fish, animals and birds, and had finally learned to organize itself into man. Man, on his part, was pushing himself forward into different aspects of existence by means of union and organization with other men.Why? Heaven only knew... Why should he complain, why worry, why speculate? - the world was going steadily forward of its own Volition whether he would or no. Truly it was. [54]

So whether somebody is able to join in or no, the world definitely proceeds on its own without any hindrances as such. In framing his "theory of existence" Lester also believes that fate which is strong and powerful definitely interferes and asserts itself in all affairs. Lester grasps the fact understood that society or the "public conviction" are more forceful than his individual opinions.The idea of something spiritual existing to pace and guide all activity on the universe is thus elucidated right from the being. Not only Lester but even Jennie Gerhardt expounds the same philosophy that the world is a beautiful place, but there is some supreme spirit supervising and cordinating all activity on earth. Jennie is not an erudite scholar and so does not know what history, physics, chemistry, botany, geology and sociology are.

> Instead there was the feeling that the world moved in some strange, unstable way.Apparently no one knew clearly what it was all about. People were born and died. Some believed that the world had been made six thousand years before; some that it was millions of year old. Was it all blind chance or was there some guiding intelligence, - a God? Almost inspite of herself she felt that there must be something -a higher power which produced all

> the beautiful things - the flowers, the stars, the trees, the grass. Nature was so beautiful! If at times life seemed cruel, yet this beauty still persisted.The thought comforted her; she fed upon it in her hours of secret loneliness.[55]

The knowledge of history , chemistry and physics does not bring about this scholarly revelation. This revelation occurs to an ordinary washer woman's daughter who slowly rises to find a place for herself amidst aristocrats. Dreiser had always been attracted towards and encouraged thinkers who could unravel the mystery of life to him and explicate the purpose of man's existence on earth as it were .The main problem about life on earth is the existence of class, gender, family and traditions. In both *Sister Carrie* and *Jennie Gerhardt* two young woman struggle hard to rise and find a place in society. Stifled by poverty theirs is an attempt to ascend socially but unfortunately society is not ready to help them in the process.In a poem entitled "Myth of possessions" Dreiser has pointed out how difficult it is to get what one desires.

> In a castle of prosperity
> A thousand servants
> In a castle of prosperity
> Possessions
> Flowers
> Walks
> Trees
> The company of those who delight in thinking on possessions,
> Yet contemplate only
> That which can not and will not be possessed
> That fades and flies
> Even as they who stand and gaze
> Or dream
> Are dreaming of that
> Which will not fade
> Or fly.[56]

This poem is true of both Carrie and Jennie Gerhardt. For

Carrie who has aspired to rise higher and higher, all that which she thinks would afford her happiness do not actually do so but only move further and further away from her and she is left with nothing but to dream of and wait for "that halcyon day when she should be led forth among dreams become real."[57] True to the spirit of the age, Sister Carrie aspires for more and more. Dreiser's opinion is that only unhappiness would be her lot.To her "peace and beauty" are something which glimmered far off and the nearer she is to them the further they appeared. She is living in a materialistic world of illusions and there is no escape from it.

As for Jennie's dreams somehow she does not possess the one and only soul with whom she has a spiritual affinity. On Lester's death Jennie feels as if a part of herself is lost. "He had been a part of her thought and feeling so long that it seemed now as though a part of herself had died."[58] For Jennie, Lester's death is a total irreparable loss. He had given her a home, her parents were happy because of the luxurious residence he had given them, her brothers and sisters were also well cared for because he had given Jennie enough money to support them all. In return Jennie had generously given her own self, her soul, her spirit and had become an indispensable part of him. But all that was not to be. Unfortunately Jennie's fate is controlled not by her but by society "She was never a master of her fate. Others invariably controlled."[59]Thus the struggle for existence of both Dreiser's heroines continues and before both of them, "Was stretching a vista of lonely years"[60] at which they were steadily gazing.

In this stage we find that Dreiser is confused with the world and is of the opinion that men and women are born in this world and while some struggle to make an existence, there are others who have the advantage of being born in rich families. If such is the case then life as such is quite disappointing for some, while for others life seems to be a pleasant experience. With this view, Dreiser proceeded to explore and peek into the life of the so called Superman so as understand his actual condition in society.

NOTES AND REFERENCES

[1] Dreiser, *The Color of a Great City* (New York: Boni and Liveright, 1923), 99.

[2] Dreiser, *Sister Carrie* (New York: Airmont Publishing Co., 1967}, 11. Subsequent references are to the same edition.

[3] Dreiser, *Sister Carrie*, 81.

[4] Dreiser, *Sister Carrie*, 21.

[5] Dreiser, *Sister Carrie*, 82.

[6] Dreiser, *Sister Carrie* ,128.

[7] Dreiser, *Sister Carrie*, 205.

[8] Dreiser, *Sister Carrie*, 252.

[9] Dreiser, *Sister Carrie* , 484.

[10] Dreiser, *Sister Carrie*, 554.

[11] Philip Gerber, *Theodore Dreiser Revisited* (New York : Twayne's United States Authors Series,1992), 33.

[12] Dreiser, *Sister Carrie*,557.

[13] Dreiser, *Jennie Gerhardt*, (Britain: O.U.P., 1992), 23. Subsequent references are to this edition, unless otherwise indicated.

[14] Dreiser, *Jennie Gerhardt*, 24.

[15] Dreiser, *Jennie Gerhardt*, 108.

[16] Dreiser, *Jennie Gerhardt*, 116.

[17] Dreiser, *Jennie Gerhardt*, 137.

[18] Dreiser, *Jennie Gerhardt*, 155.

[19] Dreiser, *Jennie Gerhardt*, 12-13.

[20]Dreiser, *Jennie Gerhardt*, 216.

[21]Dreiser, *Jennie Gerhardt,* 119.

[22]Dreiser, *Jennie Gerhardt*, 215.

[23]Dreiser, *Jennie Gerhardt,* 215.

[24]Pfizer,*The Novels of Theodore Dreiser*, 117.

[25]Dreiser, *Jennie Gerhardt*, 214.

[26]Dreiser, *Jennie Gerhardt*, 356.

[27]Dreiser, *Jennie Gerhardt*, 173.

[28]Dreiser, *Jennie Gerhardt*, 342.

[29]Dreiser, *Jennie Gerhardt*, 359.

[30]Dreiser, *Jennie Gerhardt,* 262.

[31]Dreiser, *Jennie Gerhardt*, 264.

[32]Gerber, *Theodore Dreiser Revisited,* 24.

[33]Dreiser, *Jennie Gerhardt,* 119.

[34]Dreiser, *Jennie Gerhardt*, 95.

[35]Dreiser, *Sister Carrie*, 28.

[36]Dreiser, *Sister Carrie*, 29-30.

[37]Dreiser, *Sister Carrie,* 70.

[38]Dreiser, *Sister Carrie,* 71.

[39]Dreiser, *Sister Carrie* , 56.

[40]Dreiser,*Sister Carrie*, 83.

[41]Dreiser, *Sister Carrie*, 128.

[42]Dreiser, *Sister Carrie*, 259.

[43]Dreiser, *Sister Carrie*, 226-227.

[44]Dreiser, *Jennie Gerhardt,* 17.

[45]Dreiser, *Jennie Gerhardt,*262.

[46]Dreiser, *Hey Rub -A -Dub -Dub*, 5.

[47]Dreiser, *Hey Rub -A -Dub -Dub*, 5.

[48]Dreiser ,*Jennie Gerhardt,* 17.

[49]Dreiser, *Jennie Gerhardt*, 200.

[50]Dreiser, *Jennie Gerhardt,* 289.

[51]Dreiser, *Jennie Gerhardt,* 207.

[52]Dreiser,"Neurotic America and the Sex Impulse"from *Hey Rub-A-Dub-Dub*, 141.

[53]Dreiser, *Jennie Gerhardt*, 264.

[54]Dreiser,*Jennie Gerhardt*, 345.

[55]Dreiser, *Jennie Gerhardt*, 346.

[56]Dreiser, *Moods,* 346.

[57]Dreiser, *Sister Carrie* , 382.

[58]Dreiser, *Jennie Gerhardt,* 361.

[59]Dreiser, *Jennie Gerhardt,* 363.

[60]Dreiser, *Jennie Gerhardt,* 367.

CHAPTER - III

The Financier, The Titan and The Stoic
Survival of the Strongest

Theodore Dreiser was a deep thinker and the mystery of the universe was something which kept him puzzled. The whole world was accepted by Dreiser as it is, with all its mystery. He never tried to solve them. "Solutions destroy mystery and that is why Dreiser was so hesitant to believe in any of them."[1]

Dreiser's philosophy thus concerns the universe, man's place in the universe and the make up of human personality. He is of the stern view that man should not cling to a religion, method of living or to some morals but should be able to change as and when occasion demands. In the book, *Hey Rub-A-Dub-Dub* Dreiser has given examples from newspaper articles to prove how there are no single definite solutions to life's problems for instance,

> It is immoral, unchristian and illegitimate to have a child without a husband, yet when six hundred thousand men are withdrawn from England to fight the Germans and twenty thousand virgins become war brides, it is proposed to legalize the children on the ground that it is nevertheless moral to preserve the nation from extinction.[2]

Thus pondering on the mystery, wonder and terror of life, Dreiser is convinced that there is no permanent or absolute solution to life. Everything is flexible and changes according to the situation - morals are relative. Influenced by Darwin, Dreiser believed in the inherent capacity of man to become a "Caesar, Shakespeare, Hannibal or a Leonardo."[3] This would definitely emerge within the scheme of things in the universe. "What life does is to develop and train especial inherent capacities an eye, a hand, a taste, a smell perhaps. . ."[4] but the instinct has to be innate. Even though man has developed and organized himself into societies wishing to suppress the strong, innate impulse or motivating force ultimately it is found that the theory of "Survival of the fittest" reigns supreme.Once while conversing about Spain, Dreiser's observation is as follows:

> My absolute conviction, said Dreiser, is that there is now an economic and financial understanding between financiers of all countries where there is wealth and they are all for the fascist form of government, as opposed to the democratic or communistic. They want to fascinize the world, put the poor dope at the bottom and a select few at the top. In other words, the next Caesar will be a financial Caesar.[5]

This quotation is indicative of the fact as to how far the financiers have become powerful in this world. Power and money synchronize with each other to such an extent that they almost sound synonymous as far as their then connotation is concerned.

In *Hey Rub-A-Dub-Dub* in the essay entitled "Change" Dreiser observation is follows: "We build up rules where with life is to be governed, and behold! - some fine day the character of life itself changes and our rules are worthless."[6] Given such limitations of the impermanence of things, and survival of the fittest Man, Dreiser counsels man to Perfection by advising him in the following manner, wherein, Dreiser has made clear his view that even though man is like a waif in nature he should struggle hard and proceed forward, instead of feeling depressed and hopeless. " The important thing for him to do supposing that he could, would be to avoid henceforth all destroying notions of this character and to think of himself as a waif . . and by his own effort make his own pathetic way in the world."[7] The fact that man is acted upon by forces beyond his control is further explicated in the following observation by Dreiser in his essay, "Equation Inevitable" in *Hey Rub-A-Dub-Dub* :

In the face of all the schemes and contrivances whereby

> man may live in harmony with his neighbour, there is the contrary fact that all those things are constantly being interfered with, by contrary forces, decays, mistaken notions, dreams which produce disharmony ,therefore the fact is clear that there would be a constant change and re-adjustment of forces with one another.[8]

Dreiser uses the word "chemisms" to denote all phenomena; to him:-"...Life is a chemism, personality is chemism, the emotions are chemisms."[9] The basic urge of lower animals as well as human beings 1s one and the same thing. As far as society is concerned, there are innumerable forces working at loggerheads at each other and the fittest comes out wholesome and successful. The stronger powerful ones move ahead like giants and the younger ones either get crushed or work under the stronger ones. This social Darwinism influenced Dreiser quite strongly and is reflected in his trilogy:- *The Financier* , *The Titan* and *The Stoic* .

In these novels one can trace Dreiser's Cosmic Consciousness and its " mixture of despair and idealism, of wonder and fear, of pity and guilt, of chemistry and intuition."[10] Whether one seeks power, peace, art or security one has to meet some rival forces and some friendly ones which guide him in the right direction. In "Dreiser "An Inconsistent Mechanist" by Eliseo Vivas, the writer has observed that Dreiser's observation of society is that

> it is made up of a number of sub societies arranged hierarchically in terms of power and wealth, and in each one of these ,sub- divisions the same pattern repeats itself. Within each group there are honors to be gained, privileges to be obtained and so on.[11]

Amongst all such groups of human beings is a group of cold, calculating, selfish lot known as financiers. In his essay entitled "The American Financier" in *Hey Rub-A-Dub-Dub* Dreiser refers to Vanderbilts, Goulds, J.P.Morgan and J.D.Rockefeller and explains how all of them were,absolutely opposed to democracy in practice, yet as " useful an implement for its accomplishment as for autocracy; either ignorant or contemptuous of ethical niceties... moral and immoral sexually...wise and generous in the matter of large, even universal benefactions, yet guilty of the meanest subterfuge where their own interests are concerned and seeking always to perpetuate their own fame."[12]

Dreiser has referred to Myers *History of Great American Fortunes*, Vol. II P.172 and given real life examples of "American Financiers" in *Hey Rub-A-Dub-Dub,* and has explained their dealings with society; not only did these financiers cheate society, but they also had the audacity to cheat the Government itself for their own personal profit.

> Cornelius Vanderbilt blackmailed the U. S. Steamship Company, plying between New York and California, in the amount of nearly $500,000 a year by threatening to operate a rival line.[13] J.P Morgan Senior at the outbreak of the Civil War sold the Government five hundred of its own condemned rifles for twenty two dollars each, after having but the moment before bought them from the Government for 3 dollars 50 cents each, and that with money borrowed on the strength of the proposed contract.[14]
>
> Not only did these Financiers thrive themselves but financial supremacy had become a family affair with them, that they very boldly expressed their views in social and financial matters.

> ...The supremacy of the lords of money, the Morgans, Rock fellers, du Ponts, plus the social and economic supremacy of their heirs and assigns-their children who never created or developed anything, but who, because of inherited means and names, now step forward to say who shall be first and who last in social and financial economy.[15]

Dreiser somehow could not digest the fact that while some had to work hard for their daily bread, others just inherited a great fortune and had to do nothing to make a living. Dreiser somehow felt that this was unfair.

With such an in depth analysis of financiers in mind, Dreiser transports us from the absolute helplessness of *Sister Carrie* and *Jennie Gerhardt* to the life of a powerful money baron in The *Financier, The Titan, The Stoic* trilogy. It appears that Dreiser was influenced by Nietzchean philosophy that only a superman can help in improving the conditions of human life. This attitude continues in the larger part of *The Titan* also but in the end of *The Titan* , Dreiser convinces us with a slight change in philosophy, that, in society not only does a single man stride over the world but also sometimes the masses unite to defame and oust the solitary giant. "But for him (Cowperwood) also the eternal equation- the paths of the discovery that even giants are pygmies, and that an ultimate balance must be struck."[16]

In the third part of the trilogy *The Stoic* Dreiser revives The Titan once again to power and shows that men with immense energy will always rise up from some direction or other and the only way in which they can be suppressed is by death. The material for his trilogy was from Dreiser's records of the life of Charles T. Yerkes, an industrialist who moved on to Chicago after a notorious career in Philadelphia. In Chicago, Yerkes maintained a street railway business and also dominated a corrupt city council for a decade and flourished by bribing alder men and getting things done.

In *The Financier* the first part of the trilogy the protagonist is Frank Algernon Cowperwood. At the very beginning of the novel The Financier we are told of Cowperwood's father's opinion on life.

> He looked upon life as a business situation or deal with everybody born as more or less capable machines to take part in it. It was surprising to him to see how many incapable or unsatisfactory machines there were, but, thank Heaven, now that he was getting along fairly well, this was no affair

of his.[17]

Even as a child Frank observes that as his father progresses from clerk, to teller, to Vice President of a bank, each house into which they move is one storey higher than the other. Also with the upward progression one needs to develop a different set of "connections" (P.10) to help him forge ahead in society. The observant and intelligent child Frank imagines himself "a born leader" and wants to know something about "economics" and "politics"(P.10).

Listening to his father with a greedy ear he very soon understands how life is organized and what people are doing in this world. The answers to these questions he gets from a fish tank. There is a Lobster and also a squid in the tank and the Lobster has the squid as prey. So this gives him the answer to the question:-

> "How was life organized?"
> "Things lived on each other -that was it.
> Lobsters lived on squids. What lived on
> Lobsters? Men of course... Sure that was
> it."
> "And what lived on men?" he asked himself.
> "Was it other MEN?" [18]

Here he gets his first clear notion of Darwin's philosophy of "Survival of the fittest" Growing up Frank observes that: "Men schemed and planned and then they reaped big profits. ..When he grew up Frank told himself he was going to be a broker or a financier or a banker and do some of these things."[19] Thus initiated, by the age of fifteen Frank Cowperwood begins exploring money as a commodity .The main purpose behind his exploration is that "He wanted to make himself so secure financially that even lack of quick thinking later on, would not subject him to distress and regret."[20]

Frank begins by exploring the secret of the trade. He begins to see clearly what was meant by money as a medium of exchange and how all values are calculated, according to one primary value that of gold, "If gold were high or scarce, money was said to be tight, and times were bad. If gold was plentiful, money was easy, credits were large and business was flourishing."[21] He Is a financier by instinct. Frank understands that, by controlling money he is actually controlling society. Therefore he learns all the subtleties of the stock market system which later on stands him in good stead.

A "bull" he learns is one who bought in anticipation of a higher price to come and if he is "loaded up" , with a "line" of stocks he is said to be "long" .He sells to "rea l ize" his profit, or if his margins are exhausted he is "wiped out"[22] Unfortunately Cowperwood does not rea l ize that he is work l ng contrary to the general notions of a businessman. A businessman or trader is one who manufactured and supplied goods, but here Cowperwood is actually not trading but stock jobbing or in other words speculating and gaining money not by honest but dishonest means.

Knowing the tricks of his trade Cowperwood soon senses that the sel l ing of stocks, bonds and loan certificates also necessitated creation of "manufactured fluctuations" and the watered stock is "unloaded" on the "outsiders" while "the inside ring"[23] "makes all the profit without taking any risks. Also he understands the fact that the city treasury did not need any loans, except to profit the city politicians.

With all the knowledge needed to become an expert business magnate, Cowperwood strides forward, plotting, acting and forging ahead. By the time he is thirty four years of age, he has "a banking business estimated at nearly two million dollars" and " personal holdings aggregating nearly half a million."[24] Unfortunately the panic created by the Chicago fire in 1871 brings down his holding by revealing the fact that he has tampered with funds in the city treasury in Philadelphia. His lack of foresight brings about his financial collapse, trial and imprisonment.

The prison scene makes Cowperwood drift into obscurity and become miserable. Cowperwood feels that he "was being cut out of human affairs as much as it was possible for him to be cut out."[25] Cowperwood loses his identity as he is not called by his name but is called by his convict number! The uniformity in dress and labour make him feel isolated and he desperately longs to be out. It would be worthy to note that Cowperwood was actually once proud of his "well-made clothes." "He looked bright and cheery in his well made clothes of English tweed."[26]

Once out, the individual in him is revived once again and he becomes a business tycoon once again. In 1873 Cowperwood makes a profitable deal of Jay Cooke and Co.'s collapse and regains his own fortune by selling short in a falling market and waiting for stocks to decline before buying for delivery, manages to become a millionaire once again.

In the end of the *The Financier* Cowperwood moves west to gain greater freedom of action and thought. Dreiser has himself stated in his book "Tragic America", "The tempo of this great land is one of speed and contention."[27] This mad rush for power leads to neurosis and suicidal tendencies. But still men do fight to reach the top and become invincible. Cowperwood is also no exception. Moving to Chicago, in the second part of the trilogy ,*The Titan,* Cowperwood wields power and manipulates all situations to suit his needs. Cowperwood gains a number of franchises for gas distribution. His mastery of business tactics bribery, chicanery and underhand deals make him a bright and successful businessman.

> The race is to the swift, he said to himself over and over. Yes, and the battle is to the strong. He would test whether the world would trample him underfoot or no.[28]

In another instance Cowperwood has observed, "The weaklings had to die." [29] This knowledge enables him to forge ahead very confidently as a strong man would do. Cowperwood first plans to combine three gas companies. He faces a great deal of political rivalry in this project but it is sorted out by a very simple philosophy: "Starve and beat a dog on the one hand; wheedle, pet and hold meat in front of it on the other and it can soon be brought to perform." [30] Cowperwood,was confident that "Money was the first thing to have-a lot of it. Then you secured the reputation. The two things were like legs on which you walked."[31]

In *The Titan* Cowperwood exploits the stock market with expertise. There is a reference to Cowperwood as a "virus" (P.124) which can spread quickly and destroy whole nations. There are other references to him as "Ulysses" in *The Stoic* (P.88) and he is referred to as fighting his enemies. With Trojan vigour and complacency," (*The Titan P.56)* Cowperwood plans to buy "American Match" shares at one fifty on loan, sell them at two twenty and when it crumbles to buy them back at one fifty or less and pocket his profit. Executing his deal as per plans Cowperwood makes millions in the bargain. The smaller fry denounce him as "buccaneer", "pirate" and "wolf". But all this does not affect him in the least and Cowperwood achieves his goal in life buying houses, lands, equipages, paintings and government bonds of the purest gold value .Here it would be appropriate to quote Dreiser's opinion on financiers such as J.P.Morgan, H.H.Rogers, Thomas F.Ryan or William C.Whitney. Such financiers could swallow up whole communities whole and alive, if not resisted.

> Seen at close range they are more suggestive of sharks and we of sniveling blue-fish and it is plainly to our best interests either to keep out of their way or unite firmly to oppose them in whatever way we can, unless we choose to be promptly eaten. [32]

A well developed taste for art seems to accompany his rise in status. Cowperwood also begins his collection with a picture of "rude odalisques", another brilliant picture of "Gerome" and a portrait of Aileen by a Dutch artist Ian Van Beers. Later on Perugino, brilliant examples of Luini, Previtali and Pintirrichio are added on to it. Even the house is remodified as soon as there is a rise in his status "fence -sharp pointed, gray palings was an abomination"[33].

Cowperwood has an eye for detail and was quite choosy and artistic in his choice. With the advance in monetary position his ideas regarding women also begin to change . "He had little faith in the ability of women aside from their value as objects of art."[34] Cowperwood divorces his first wife to marry his boss' daughter Aileen because she is charming and more vibrant, sociable and outgoing. But he is not enthusiastic about his relationship with Aileen, for soon he begins looking for a woman with "keener artistic perceptions."[35] With this attitude he begins philandering with married women, prostitutes, secretaries and so on. He begins feeling that women were objects of aesthetic pleasure and that he should have the pleasure to choose according to his satisfaction. So he associates with many women -Rita Sohlberg, Mrs. Josephine Ledwell, Dorothy Ormsby, Jessie Belle Hinsdale, Toma Lewis, Hilda Jewell and so on. Cowperwood's belief in the chemistry of life encourages him and prods him on. It is his power and fame which draw women to him; they do not seem to love him really.

Scenes of material disharmony abound in the book as every time Aileen spies him with a new woman she would naturally throw tantrums threatening to kill the other woman, or Cowperwood, or both. Ultimately finding him engrossed in Berenice Fleming, Aileen attempts to commit suicide but is saved by Cowperwood.

Cowperwood is not all successful in life as rival forces also keep operating side by side. As Dreiser has himself made an observation regarding the spirit of America at that time in *A Hoosier Holiday* "It was just entering on the vast, splendid, most lawless and most savage period in which the great financiers, ...were plotting and conniving the enslavement of people and belaboring each other for power."[36]

It is thus natural that some others try to stifle Cowperwood's rise. So when he contests the elections for the post of City treasurer, men like Kerrigan and Tiernan also consider themselves eligible for the post and they do not allow him to succeed. Cowperwood's fight for the post becomes a tough one and charged of bribery and corruption Cowperwood loses his place in the City Council.In the *American Financier* Dreiser writes that the individual and the mass, " are interdependent facts and one cannot escape the other , try as each may"[37]. The individual has to understand that he shares his world with others and sometimes the individual may arrive at the foreground and at other times society pushes the individual to the background" as it happens in *The Titan.* Anyhow economic dealings were always concerned with society and Dreïser was quite aware of this fact. Dreiser was also of the view that money should be equally distributed so that there would not be a great deal of imbalance in society. "There is a social unbalance here which would not permit of any sane picture that did not clearly reflect social unbalance."[38]

As far as Cowperwood is concerned the ultimate balance which gets struck, is only for the time being, as, very soon, he starts planning newer ventures as his heart hungers for more wealth. Having wrecked lives of two women and a score of other victims, Cowperwood is not satisfied and we find that in the third part of the trilogy, Cowperwood guided by his natural bent of mind exposes newer pastures.

In the third part of the trilogy, *The Stoic* ,Cowperwood undauntedly forges ahead scheming a method of unifying and modernizing the London underground traction system. Berenice Fleming's devotion to him as his mistress and her aiding him in renewing faith in himself helps him to become a great financier once again and take up gigantic projects. Whenever Cowperwood has difficulties in competing with his rivals to gain control of the lines he follows his usual technique : "Dangle enough cash before the eyes of the quarreling investors, and whatever their objections, it was more than likely that they would take the cash and let quarrel go."[39]

To Cowperwood religion is something which the weak in mind and spirit resort to. The strong do not need God or anyone to help them in their endeavours, their own intelligence and craftiness is enough

> Had there ever been such a thing as an indubitably noble soul? He was scarcely prepared to believe it. Men killed

> to live-all of them-and wallowed in lust in order to reproduce themselves. In fact, wars, vanities, pretenses, cruelties, greed, lusts, murder, spelled their true history with only the weaklings running to God for aid. And the strong using this belief in God to further the conquest of the weak.[40]

So, tactfully scheming, Cowperwood wishes to get Aileen out of the way, in order to proceed with his relationship with Berenice. So he very craftily and cunningly engages one of his men Tollifer to attend on her, socially engage and entertain her. Not only with his business rivals, but even with his wife he knows how to side track them and proceed with his interests. In the midst of all these affairs Cowperwood grows old and dies of Bright's Disease. Cowperwood is not all selfish and mean during his life time. He has his generous side too-he wishes to leave his treasured art gallery to the public. He builds a tomb-a canopy of ancient Greek design for himself and his dear wife Aileen. This is symbolic of his enduring and everlasting reciprocation for Aileen's selfless sacrifice and service in those hard times when he was imprisoned in Philadelphia.

Cowperwood also plans to build a hospital in New York but unfortunately it doesn't get built before his death. Even in his death he remains a lonely man with his wife Aileen deserting him on seeing Berenice.His "unheralded funeral cortege"[41] is sent by the doctor's advise to Aileen's house.In *Jennie Gerhardt* ,Jennie is the lone mourner during Lester's death, here we have Berenice Fleming as the lone sufferer and mourner at Cowperwood's death, though Aileen joins in a little later. His death is followed by payment of litigation, assessment, taxes and his great mansion and art collection, everything that belongs to him gets auctioned off to pay the claims. This is true of Yerkes' story also. Just as Yerkes had looted in life, his house and belongings were looted in death. Soon Aileen also dies of pneumonia.

Dreiser has actually narrated the story of Cowperwood not so much to talk of Cowperwood but to deal with the condition of society as such. Aspiring for more than what one can reach naturally breeds contempt and ill-health in society.

> Not only is the whole energy of our lives turned into a miserable struggle for the unattainable, namely, the uninterrupted and complete gratification of our desires, but our hearts are soured and our nature warped by the grimness of the struggle.Life is made bitter. The natural hunger of the heart for righteous relationship is stifled. We become harsh, cold, indifferent.[42]

It is perceivable that Cowperwood has no pricking of moral conscience and is therefore a hardened, insensitive creature, not a human being. To what use? Inspite of all the wealth and luxury he has once enjoyed he is left to die alone in a very pathetic condition. To counteract such ruthless human beings, there are other softer, humanitarian creatures like Berenice who try to do something for the uplift of the deprived and wretched ones in society.

The growth and transformation of Berenice from a totally materialistic girl who loves Cowperwood for his money to a spiritually elevated benefactress is superbly portrayed by Dreiser. Berenice turns into a yogi in the concluding chapters. The lady who decided to be Cowperwood's mistress with hopes of inheriting his property later on turns out to be a spiritually awakened soul who understood the fact that: "there was something about the limited thought of the self that was lost in the larger thought of the not self that brought about forgetfulness of self in the nervous person and so health."[43]

Thus there is a gradual spiritual development and she understands the meaning of Brahma, and ultimately realizes that peace and happiness can be attained only through universal love. "You are the soul of the universe. If a man come to your door, go and meet yourself.For all are one. The idea of separateness is hallucination." [44]Universal love can be achieved only through renunciation, sounds quite contradictory but quite true all the same.

The bhakti's renunciation is easy, smooth flowing and as

> natural as thing around us.A man loves his own city , then he begins to love his country, and the intense love for his little city drops off, smoothly,naturally. Again, a man learns to love the whole world; his love for his country, his intense fanatical patriotism drops off, without hurting him without any manifestation of violence.[45]

Ultimately having gained supreme knowledge from India she returns to New York to hear that all Cowperwood's property had been auctioned off. With a heavy heart she finishes off the unfinished task of Cowperwood, that of building a hospital for neglected children. In this task she uses up half of all her possessions. Thus she tries to relieve the suffering of at least a few unfortunate children in the world. "A drop in the ocean was her contribution. One drop."[46]

So we find that for the most part the trilogy is dominated by the towering personality of Frank Algernon Cowperwood-the Superman; who is presented to the readers with all his weakness and positive aspects. As Philip Gerber has observed,

> Dreiser's main purpose was to -draw Cowperwood as I see him. . .And when I get through with him he'll stand there, unidealised and uncursed, for you ...to take and judge according to your own lights and blindnesses and attitudes towards life.[47]

Explaining the problems which could ensue suddenly in business activities, for instance Dreiser gives an example of stock market. He clearly elucidates how crashes occur in the stock market like the one which occurred in *The Financier* , thus rendering homeless thousands of people.

> The stock market and hence all employment proceeds by cycles. Thus,betimes stocks are active, yet selling at a reasonable figure, and at that time there is very little unemployment. But business increasing, stocks rise, and then new issues are floated. That . . . inspires hundreds of factories and building projects. Men work overtime . .

> and at such times stocks invariably sell several hundred percent above their actual value . . It leaps! ..The banks at such times permits borrowing and borrowing and borrowing to everyone . . . The result, of course - as in 1873, 1891, 1907 and 1928- is violent inflation and also, of course, inevitable crash.[48]

What a gross national loss. Such periods are periods of irrevocable depression to thousands and thousands of people. Some mentally strong creatures are able to come out of the mess but others fail irremediably. By underhand deals and secret agreements magnates like the Rockefeller create a competition in which less powerful individuals are shifted and suppressed and in due course many workers also lose their jobs and are trampled by the stronger ones. Such is the case of Cowperwood also who rises higher and higher only to suppress others.

There is exploitation, underhand dealings and the like in business that Dreiser is rather fuming at the audacity and tactfulness of such businessmen. Dreiser has taken great pains to elaborate on the variety of methods which businessmen use to cheat people. They sometimes force out money from their less fortunate brethren.

> An example of "By Force" in this sense concerns some of our big railroads and their schemes to get control of the rich coal mines in their area, mainly by changing such preposterous freight rates to independent coal operators as to make it impossible for them to compete with other companies. In lawsuits afterwards, it has been brought out that these independent companies could not fulfill their contracts because the railroads claimed there were no cars available in which to ship their coal."[49]

Such are the techniques used to force companies to submit or fallout of competition with the bigger tycoons. They employ all sorts of tactics to win their way out successfully. According to law, "man cannot make a contract with himself. Yet the directors of one corporation can make a lawful contract with another corporation of which they are also directors." [50]

This law is naturally bound to be misused and lead to the greatest frauds. By such contracts the fraudulent businessmen make exorbitant payments for things which do not exist at all, because the same man is director of the various companies with which he manages contracts! Atrocious and vile methods are applied to make the maximum profit in minimum time while fooling both the government and the common man with regard to policies adopted by them.

Such deals by Rockefellers or Carnegies dupe many young Americans to visualize themselves in the same situation. As Dreiser has himself expressed in *A Book About Myself* , which according to Lehan is a revelation of his own sense of self, when he took flight into fancy and identified himself with Yerkes. "To be president or vice president or something , some great thrashing business of some kind. Great God, how sublime it seemed!"[51]

Even though it seems as if Dreiser himself was lured into the net. Dreiser brushed aside the notion as he only found more of corruption than anything else in business. Quite surprisingly such great businessman also appeared quite religious and they generously gave donations to the church.

The Puritans in America considered gaining more and more wealth was Lord's blessings; something divine and heavenly. By gaining more and more wealth the Puritans felt that they were becoming spiritually superior beings. These misapprehensions and biased opinions was all the more reason for the craze for more wealth. It was considered something prestigious to be able to afford living in a costly apartment or in a posh hotel. Dreiser had himself longed for it many time. In *Dawn* , Dreiser expresses this view , "My brain was fairly bubbling with ideas of still greater grandeur to come, in short,how I might climb and climb until even the best hotels would not be beyond me and I could walk unashamed and untroubled in the best theaters... money in my pocket, a sense of real ability and fitness to live enfolding me as a cloak."[52]

So, if Cowperwood aspired above his reach, it was not his own fault. It was the fault of the society which dreamt of such ideal conditions, and in the process, the stronger ones resorted to ruthless exploitation of the weak and unsuccessful. The Successful heroes were actually idealized, glorified and looked upon as a thing worth emulating by the less successful. Therefore Cowperwood's behavior also seems to be in keeping with the myths of his time. The trilogy is actually satirising the behaviour of the people of America of his time .

Moreover not only their own efforts but some such aid which they inherit as legacy also aid these men in becoming successful. Cowperwood inherits a legacy of fifteen thousand dollars. Contrary to the heroic notions of his admirers, Cowperwood just makes money by cheating. He himself feels that "They were all Hawks-he and they. They were all tigers facing each other in a financial `jungle."[53] Here it is important to note that Dreiser has actually blamed the society for the success of Cowperwood.

These organizations are never dominated by One man alone. They grow like a rank growth of weeds in a small community. They fatten and are added to until, if you attempt to trace them out, you reach by wider and ever-widening circles the very body and blood of the people themselves.

> We are all sinners, either directly or indirectly, if no more than by the fact that we do not protest. If we do not protest, it is evident that this idea is not so very shocking to us, certainly not enough to irritate us to the point of protesting.[53]

So beautifully has Dreiser pointed out that if we the society fail to resist exploitation then exploitation would definitely continue. In his *Notes on life* also Dreiser has pointed out the fact that the duty of society is to stop such "corporate masters." If not they will stop the country's progress or at least the country's democratic process, is what Dreiser feels about them. "As such there is not room for them (corporate masters) in any scheme or dream of democracy. They will and must be stopped by those who believe that democracy is possible and that it is a humanely agreeable relationship to be maintained, or they will stop democracy.[54] Proceeding ahead in the same passage, Dreiser has pointed out that as long as there are others who are ready to be subservient and call them lord and master these stronger and crafty men will naturally forge ahead and claim their incentives from society and maybe they might get the lion's share, because they are quite powerful. Then in such a case the law of the jungle would also hold good in this universe. To quote Dreiser:

> Today, on the lips of almost all Americans are such words as the chief, the big fellow, the boss, the king of this or that from potatoes to oil companies and, instead of open statements of belief and confessions of faith in a simpler and more equitable world, there are all too many whisperings as to the danger, as to the limiting power of such things on strong,creative men and their right to incentive.[55]

By such "things" Dreiser is referring to 'social reforms'. As long as an awareness is not created in the minds of society, such businessmen and corporate masters would definitely forge ahead to the distress of all less capable individuals. Dreiser gives the readers some bit of advice as to how to succeed if at all one wished to succeed. It is not by being inactive and lazy but by using one's mind to think. If one does not think at all one cannot help but face failure in life. Describing Cowperwood's philosophy of life Dreiser states :

> he appeared at times a little bit removed and superior or distant, but solely because he was thinking . Even at this early age he was a keen judge of men There were the weak and the strong, Physically and mentally, some men were destined for success by their temperament-that he could see; others were cut out for failure by the same

> token. You could not expect a brief spindling, half constructed figure of a man with no brain and no forceto cut a figure in the world, and you could not possibly expect a great dynamic soul like Steemberger not to be heard of. [56]

The most important aspect which distinguishes a successful man from an unsuccessful one, is that the successful man is a thinker. The same idea occurs over and over again in the text.

> He thought, thought, thought all the time, in prosperity and in times when he was not so prosperous. He based everything on thought, after he made due allowance for chance and opportunity, which he could not control. He would have agreed with Machiavelli that, other things being equal, fortune is always with him who plans. .was so fatalist. . . he was no coward.[57]

So the factors which go into the making of a successful man are planning, thinking and bravery— Cowperwood has all the three. The difference between him and any other human being is that they just spent their time talking and not in thinking; that was why they are not able to perceive and grasp things as quickly as he did "people talked and talked, but they acted according to their necessities and desires only as a rule they were not quick and clever as he was."[58]

Not only is he quick and clever but he also perceives himself to be a "shrewd, calculating, thinking man." [59] Once again it is the thinking aspect which is stressed. Also it is necessary that when one starts thinking one should think positively otherwise negative thoughts will enter and ruin all plans .So here again it is noteworthy that Cowperwood is successful because he always thinks of success. "Where many men were thinking of ruin, he was thinking of success."[60]

As far as money matters are concerned Cowperwood is quite adept at handling it properly. He knows how to make money multiply. Describing his skill Dreiser observes that the following technique should be followed.

> Imagine yourself by nature versed in the art of finance, capable of playing with sum of money in the forms of stocks,certificates, bonds or better yet, imagine yourself one of those subtle masters of the mysteries of the higher forms of chess-the type of mind so well illustrated by the famous historic chess- players, who could sit with their backs to a group of rivals playing fourteen men at once, calling out all the moves in turn, remembering all the positions of all the men on all the boards, and winning. This of course would be an overstatement of the subtlety of Frank Cowperwood at this time, and yet it would not be wholly out of key. He knew instinctively what could be done with a given sum of money-how as cash it could be deposited in one place, and yet as credit and the basis of moving checks, used not in one but many other places at the same time.[61]

Dreiser's observation of the crafty methods opted by Financiers is clearly elucidated in the above passage. Manipulation of money—borrowing from someone, depositing elsewhere and making it multiply were all tricks of the trade. Cowperwood has mastered his trade to such an extent that he has grown unscrupulous in his handling. This is because of his firm faith that :

> Life was a dark, insoluble mystery; but, whatever it was, strength and weakness were its two constitutions. Strength would win; weakness lose. He must rely on swiftness of thought, accuracy, his judgment and on nothing else.[62]

Cowperwood desperately forces himself to win. As far as he is concerned he feels that he is justified in his acts; his opinion is that once a chance occurs it should not be missed.

> Time and chance happened to all men. Look at the squid he had seen. Was it its fault that it had been put in the tank with the lobster with no chance ultimately of saving its

> life? Some great, curious force was at work here throwing vast masses of people into life and they could not all succeed. Some had to fail-many. Only a few could lead. He wondered about himself-whether he was born to lead he must work; he mustn't be a spindling figure like some of these poor things about him.Never![63]

Cowperwood's capacity to hard work, to plan, think and his smart and handsome dealing are worth emulating by businessmen. But his unscrupulousness in his dealing and his corrupt underhand practices just for the sake of success. It is here that one stops admiring him because of the corrupt ways in which he gets his money. No amount of justification from Nature can justify this fact because the next question arises, whether we have really evolved into higher, spiritually elevated creatures or no. Cowperwood's nonchalant justification of his extramarital affairs and his lack of faith in any religion, whatsoever, depict the condition of the amoral society of his time. Here, Cowperwood depicts Dreiser's opinions on religions and morals. Dreiser also did not believe in either religion as it existed then or conventional morals. "Religion it was for the weak, the fearsome. Morals - those who had them had them; those who didn't didn't".[64]

Such a casual attitude would naturally shock readers, who would find it hard to accept an outright amorally materialistic attitude. Cowperwood's main obsession is with his possessions. It is an unfortunate truth that the more man possesses the more he desires, and the vicious cycle continues uninterrupted. Cowperwood's opinion is that,

> A man in a way is the shadow of his possessions and deeds, quite as much as they are a projection or reflection of him. The twain are indissolubly linked.They grow as a tree and its shade . The man is stronger for his possessions and his possessions are stronger for the man.[65]

Thus Cowperwood keeps on chasing illusions with a fixed motto of "preserving himself intact and succeeding."[65] Cowperwood has no ideas in life and is naturally lost in the wilderness of accumulation of more and more wealth, and to what end; he doesn't know. "He was seeking the realization of an ideal, yet to one's amazement our very ideals change at times and leave us floundering in the dark."[66] This directionless endeavor makes Cowperwood a fabulous figure but," his heart iron, his intentions sinister-the acme of cruel, plotting devilry."[66] It is then that society awakens in the form of his rivals who feel that somehow,

> They would not succumb to this Titan who was bent on undoing them. They would not be devoured by this gorgon of the east. He should be made to pay an honest return to the city or get out.[67]

Cowperwood who is insensitively drifting ahead is thus checked by society which has patiently tolerated him for quite a long time. As observed by Pfizer, "The social balance had swung too far in the direction of absolute power by the strong and that reform was the mechanistic response of the social organism to this imbalance."[68]

> In *The Titan* Dreiser has explained his philosophy clearly. At the ultimate remove, God or the life force, if anything, is an equation, and at its nearest expression for man- the contract social is that also. Its method of expression appears to be that of generating the individual , in all his glittering variety and scope, and through progressing to the mass with its problems. In the end a balance is invariably struck wherein the mass subdues the individual or the individual the mass. In the meantime there have sprung up social words and phrases expressing a need of balance of equation. These are right, justice, truth, morality, an honest mind, a pure heart-all words meaning: a balance must be struck. The strong must not be too strong; the weak not too weak.[69]

Dreiser is apprehensive that such a mad rush for wealth needs to be opposed or stifled or else whole nations will go crazy;

get destroyed in the process. At the end of the first book Dreiser has pointed out that if the witches in Macbeth were to foretell Cowperwood's future they would exclaim thus:- "Hail to thee Frank Cowperwood master and no master, prince of a world of dreams whose reality was sorrow."[70]

It is quite explicit that what we think is going to give us happiness is actually to be the root cause of sorrow. At the end of *The Titan,* Dreiser's comment is:

> And this giant himself. rushing on to new struggles and new difficulties in an older land;or ever suffering the goal of restless heart-for him was no ultimate peace; no real understanding, but only hunger and thirst and wonder. Wealth, wealth, wealth!...In Dresden a palace for one woman; in Rome a second for another. In London a third for his beloved Berenice; the lure of beauty ever in his eye. The lives of two women wrecked, a score of victims despoiled. . . And he resigned, and yet not-loving, understanding, doubting, caught at last by the drug of personality which he could not gainsay.[71]

Berenice is quite a worldly wise woman and hers is not an attitude of sacrificial surrender. Her expectation is that of sympathetically co operating with Cowperwood in such endeavors as would benefit both of them. Hers is a partnership with Cowperwood for attempts at success. Her attitude is as follows:-

> You are a social outcast, and so am I. The world has sought to frustrate you. In my own case, it has attempted to exclude me from the sphere to which, temperamentally and in every other way, I feel I belong.You are resentful, and so am I. Therefore,a partnership: one of beauty and strength and intelligence and courage on both sides, but without being dominated by either of us. For without fair play between us, there is no possibility of this unsanctioned union enduring.[72]

So, marriage or for that matter living together was also a matter of convenience. There is no spiritual bonding of two hearts but just a formal endeavoring or strife towards success. But there is a basic difference between the two - Cowperwood accumulates more and more mansions and loads more wealth. But Berenice's stern opinion is that: "If only she had great wealth, great power...she would never waste it on great houses and lands and show, but rather surround herself with an atmosphere which should be exquisite and, of course, inspirational."[73]

Even though there is no spiritual bonding between the two, Berenice being a very intelligent girl, knows how to make a lasting relationship with Cowperwood. "Yet because of her intellect and the sincerity of her ambition, their relationship had been based on mutual appreciation as well as affection."[74]

There is no change in Cowperwood's attitude to life even in *The Stoic.* Needing $100,000,000 for an underground railway project in London, Cowperwood first thought is of approaching financiers in America but later on decides to use his old tricks once again.

> Since his schemes were not as well-known in England as in his own country, he was more than ever bent upon organizing a company for this and a company for that, one for each branch or existing system that was to be added or done over, the watered stocks of which would be sold to a gullible public. That was the way of such things. The public could always be hoodwinked into buying anything that was made to look sufficiently promising.[75]

Ultimately all profits are to be made by fooling the public. All this is possible only because the public is ready to be fooled. Moreover Berenice always endeavours to keep him in high spirits. The following telegram sent by Berenice to Cowperwood bears testimony to this fact. "The sun shines on the England you step on. It is a silver door that opens your Greatest achievement and your greatest fame. The sea has been grey without you."[76]

Such flattering messages work to keep him in good spirits. References to Cowperwood as "Ullyses" (P.88) and "Caesar" naturally give him the boost needed to work wonders. Cowperwood's purchase of Charing Cross however invited mixed reactions. While in London the reaction is to Cowperwood's favour, the reaction in Chicago is entirely different.

> That such a ruthless trickster, So recently ejected from that city, should proceed to London, and there by reason of his wealth, cunning and general effrontery, be able to cajole the powers of that great city into looking to him for the possible solution of their transit needs, was too much![77]

Cowperwood continues to rise despite all such reports. According to his own estimate of himself, he is, "a young, ambitious American businessman trying to find his way through an English financial jungle."[78] Cowperwood's underground traction system is quite a profitable affair and he makes fast buck with it. While progressing in his business, he also wants to show that he has a great deal of interest in art collection and so without any knowledge or real love for art buys Turner's painting, 'Rockets and Blue Lights', for $78,000,[79] and hangs it in his office.

In *The Stoic*, Cowperwood experiences a change in attitude for the very first time he comprehends the uselessness of all his endeavours. On a trip to Norway, Cowperwood contrasts the peaceful atmosphere of the place with his own business entanglements. It is then that Cowperwood gets to understand how one can lead a simple life and still be happy and that it is not necessary for one to accumulate wealth in order to get happiness. What impresses him most about the entire northern scene is the fact that it represents such a sharp and socially insignificant phase of a world that really has no need for any such temperament as his. The immense oceans, supported its inhabitants by the process of supplying them with fish, and there is enough of employment to enable them to build and make habitable sufficient spaces of soil when they return, and thus round out their lives in comparative comfort. And yet he feels that these people have more from life in sheer beauty, simple comfort, and charming social customs than he and thousands of others like him who are so strenuously engaged in accumulating money.

`What really, lay ahead of him? More subway? More art galleries? More irritations due to public opinion?[80] This passage clearly outlines the fact that riches do not really bring happiness. Moreover accumulation of money through malpractice would only mean more and more problems before any could be solved. Cowperwood has actually understood the futility of accumulating wealth. It does not seem to lead him anywhere. Berenice's playful observations is also quite seriously meaningful when she states: "You have been like some big engine or machine that's tearing full speed somewhere, but doesn't know exactly where."[81]

The experience Cowperwood had in Norway actually reinforces the fact that one does not need to be a "superman" or a "big hero", "a Caesar" or a "Ulysses" in order to enjoy the simple pleasures of life on earth. With very little cash, books and music the Norwegian fisherman were having a harmonious life in close communion with nature. His business association only bought with it more craft, cunning and general depression.

The change in mind is revealed in Cowperwood's handing over his mansion as a museum for the public and the hospital which is to be built is not to be on an"expensive site".(P.256)Highly surprising that Cowperwood should think of simplicity or cheap location. The best part of the change is in Cowperwood's concern for the poor. "It is to be for the poor-not for people with money who can afford to go elsewhere-and neither race, creed, nor color are to have anything to do with the right of admission."[82]

Despite all those changes even in death Cowperwood had chalked out an identity for himself by means of his magnificent tomb. "As her carriage came into full view of the tomb, Aileen was again and finally impressed by her husband's power of self-presentation."[83]

In sheer contrast with Cowperwood's views are the views of Berenice who feels that not wealth but "the mystery and immensity of voiceless time and space"[84] is what is to be explored earnestly, so that "life would be complete and significant."[85]

As far as Berenice is concerned her life does become complete and significant when she discovers the secret of life is not in being selfish, crafty, cunning and self -centered but in sharing God's gifts with one and all. As Dreiser has himself quoted from the Bible:

We brought nothing into this world, and it is certain we can carry nothing out. The Lord gave and the Lord had taken away; blessed be the name of the Lord.[86] Vanity, pride, power and accumulated wealth are but for a short while on earth and have no significance whatsoever in the long run. The most pathetic part of the whole book is when Mrs. Aileen Cowperwood has to move out of her mansion also in order to auction it off. Actually every little bit of property has to be auctioned off to pay up to the London Under ground Company. All the pictures, rugs, tapestries and each and everything which Cowperwood had collected very lovingly, bit by bit are all auctioned off to pay the company and Aileen has to bear the brunt of it all.

In fact, the sum and substance of all those years and efforts was that she lived alone, was visited by no true friend,legally defeated in one honest claim after another, until at last she fully realized that the dream of grandeur which this house represented had vanished into thin air. ..The law and corporations and the executors, like wolves, were constantly on her trail, and finally they had caught up with her to the place where she now had to move out of her own home in order that it could be auctioned off to strangers.[87] If Cowperwood himself is crafty and cunning like a wolf - planning, plotting and scheming methods to amass wealth, there are other wolves ready to loot it from him.

> His gold stead, once owned by the king of Belgium and bought for $80,000 ; the pink marble bath tub in Aileen's bathroom,which had cost $50,000; the fabulous silk carpets from the Mosque of Ardebil; the bronzes, red African vases, Louis XIV gilt sofas; candelabras, also Louis XIV of cut crystal, with amethyst and to pay drops ;exquisite porcelain, glass, silver and smaller objects such as cameras,rings,pins, necklaces, precious stones and figurines.[88]

The list is endless, had Cowperwood known earlier that this is what it would all come to, may be he would have been generous and straight forward. Anyhow wealth accumulated by crafty means are grabbled away by other "wolves" in the same manner.

Dreiser has himself given suggestions as to how the financiers of America could have behaved instead of endlessly amassing wealth only. They are many other useful things which they would have done for the benefit of society. According to Dreiser, the living individual is worth something and anyone of our financiers might have done what no American of wealth, had done till then; invested some of his boundless wealth in personality , or endowed a wholly independent magazine or newspaper or theater, or a school of special learning free from dogmatic interference, or a publishing house, or a university. Unfortunately the strongest lack or flaw in the American

> organizing financial temperament is its inability to see either character or significance in anything save movements which tend to further the most material financial aims: railroads, butcher companies, electricity, gas, typewriter and any other purely mechanical or material organizations.[89]

Cowperwood like all other financiers has tended to further his own interests and even though nobody could effectively stop him while he is alive, they actually manage it once he passes away by grabbing and evacuating his house of all his beloved possessions and auctioning them. Dreiser had pointed it out more than once that such scheming individuals are able to exploit only because the mass is ready enough to be exploited. Only when "the organized sense of the mass becomes sufficiently intelligent for it to act in concert is it possible to sweep away or even curb the individual,"[90] and revert the situation. So as long as the mass remains dull and inactive will such financiers benefit and bloom. Once the mass is awakened, his chances of success becomes limited. As far as the financier is concerned he is a mind blazing with new ideas and he cannot rest until he has accomplished his dreams. Bubbling with enthusiasm he strives and there's no stopping him.

> To the aggressive organizing mind life is and always has been a free and practically uncharted sea. It finds itself blazing with an impulse to get some one new thing done; it conceives some great scheme, is inspired with some great enthusiasm for something and thereafter all else is as nothing.[91]

As in the case of Cowperwood this enthusiasm also is not a permanent thing. At least in old age, if not earlier, the giants begin questioning their aims in life and try analysing whether it is worth the trouble after all. Still the fact remains that once having entered business they cannot go back. They persist and face whatever else is in store for them. The struggle between the mass and the individual is a constant struggle. Dreiser's observation is that: "Like the Lilliputians, the mass as often succeeds in binding Gulliver with their threads as Gulliver succeeds in tearing through their petty ways."[92]

So it is a vicious cycle and continues to plot, scheme and topple one another. But all this is vain struggle and nothing concrete is to come out of it all. We shall be disturbing our own peace and also the peace of one another and it serves no purpose . "For man walked in a vain shadow, and disquieteth himself in vain: he heapeth up riches and cannot tell who shall gather them."[93]

This quote from the Bible is so true of Cowperwood because all the wealth which he had so painstakingly and meticulously plotted and collected were ultimately auctioned and looted by other avaricious people like him. Dreiser wishes to inspire the readers as well as all his fellow Americans to forget such materialistic endeavours and remember that this is not the purpose of our existence. If during our life time we can relieve sorrow and misery around us, that would actually enable us to be more noble and magnanimous and naturally we shall always be a coveted asset of society.

The days of our age are three score years and ten; and though men be so strong that they come fourscore years; yet is their strength then but labor and sorrow; so soon passeth it away, and we are gone.[94] However high and mighty a man might have been during his life time, ultimately one has to mingle with the lowly dust. To Berenice, who viewed from a distance, Cowperwood's tomb seemed: "High and proud, and yet small, under the protective elms grown tall around it."[95]

This statement is highly reflective of the fact that whatever experiences one has in society, it is but a minute speck when viewed in relation to the universe. So all experiences are relative, and nothing is absolute. So there is no necessity to feel proud or humiliated whatsoever. "Even our greatest individuals,. . . . are but minute factors in the total machinery, little able to forefend against disaster or the ultimate nothingness that swallows them."[96]

NOTES AND REFERENCES

[1]Lundquit, *Theodore Dreiser,* (New York: Ungar, 1974),109.

[2]Dreiser, *Hey Rub-A-Dub-Dub,*15.

[3]Dreiser, *Hey Rub-A-Dub-Dub,*107.

[4]Dreiser, *Hey Rub-A-Dub-Dub,*114.

[5]Tjader, *Dreiser: A New Dimension,*83.

[6]Dreiser,*Hey Rub-A-Dub-Dub,*21.

[7]Dreiser,*Hey Rub-A-Dub-Dub,*123.

[8]Dreiser,*Hey Rub-A-Dub-Dub,*158.

[9]Alfred Kazin and Charles Shapiro,*The Stature of Theodore Dreiser,* 123.

[10]Charles Child Walcutt, *Modern American Fiction* (O.U.P.,1963), 46.

[11]Kazin and Shapiro, *The Stature of Theodore Dreiser,*239.

[12]Dreiser, *Hey Rub-A-Dub-Dub,*74.

[13] Myers, *History of Great American Fortunes,*Vol. II (Referred to by Dreiser in his "American Financier"),120-121.

[14]Myers,172.

[15]Dreiser, *Tragic America,* (New York: Boni and Liveright, 1931),8.

[16]Dreiser, *The Titan (*Cleveland: World Publishing Co., 1946), 551.

[17] Dreiser, *The Financier(*New York: Harper,1912), 2.

[18] Dreiser, *The Financier,*13.

[19] Dreiser, *The Financier,*21.

[20] Dreiser, *The Financier,*105.

[21] Dreiser, *The Financier,*18.

[22] Dreiser, *The Financier,*80.

[23] Dreiser, *The Financier,*179.

[24] Dreiser, *The Financier,*275.

[25] Dreiser, *The Financier,*383.

[26] Dreiser, *The Financier,*53.

[27] Dreiser, *Tragic America,*1.

[28] Dreiser, *The Titan,*2.

[29] Dreiser, *The Financier,*661.

[30] Dreiser, *The Titan*,222.

[31] Dreiser, *The Financier*,777.

[32] Dreiser, *Hey Rub-A-Dub-Dub* ,84.

[33] Dreiser, *The Financier* ,112.

[34] Dreiser, *The Titan,* 118.

[35] Dreiser, *The Titan*,108.

[36] Dreiser, *A Hoosier Holiday,* (New York: John Lane, 1916), 171-172.

[37] Dreiser, *Hey Rub-A-Dub-Dub*,79.

[38] Dreiser, *Letters of Theodore Dreiser: A Selection Ed Robert Elias.* (Philadelphia: Univ. of Pennyslvania, 1959) Vol II,583.

[39]Dreiser, *The Stoic* (Cleveland: World Publishing Co., 1947), 132.

[40]Dreiser, *The Stoic,* 137.

[41]Dreiser , *The Stoic*,268.

[42]Dreiser, *A Selection of Uncollected Prose* (Unpublished Manuscript),157.

[43]Dreiser, *The Stoic*,277.

[44]Dreiser, *The Stoic*,295.

[45]Dreiser, *The Stoic*,298.

[46]Dreiser, *The Stoic*,310.

[47]Gerber, *Theodore Dreiser Revisited*,63.

[48]Dreiser, *Tragic America,* 63.

[49]Dreiser, *Tragic America*,38.

[50]Dreiser, *Tragic America*,40-41.

[51] Richard Lehan , *Theodore Dreiser: His World And His Novels* (Carbondale: Southern Illinois Univ. Press. 1969),100.

[52]Dreiser, *Dawn*,581.

[53]Dreiser,*The Financier*,354.

[54]Dreiser,*Notes on Life*,299. (Dreiser's proposed work of 40 chapters which has not taken a book form. Helen Dreiser named it Notes of Life)

[55]Dreiser, *Notes on Life*,299.

[56]Dreiser, *The Financier*,40.

[57]Dreiser, *The Financier*,432.

[58]Dreiser, *Tragic America,* 432.

[59]Dreiser, *Tragic America,* 387.

[60]Dreiser, *The Financier*,769.

[61]Dreiser, *The Financier*, 190.
[62]Dreiser, *The Financier*,476.
[63]Dreiser, *The Financier*,40-41.
[64]Dreiser, *The Financier*,187.
[65]Dreiser, *The Financier*,102.
[66]Dreiser, *The Titan*,201.
[67]Dreiser, *The Titan*,541.
[68]Pfizer, *The Novels of Theodore Dreiser*,157.
[69]Dreiser, *The Titan*,551.
[70]Dreiser, *The Financier*,780.
[71]Dreiser, *The Titan*,552.
[72]Dreiser, *The Stoic*,3.
[73]Dreiser, *The Stoic*,7.
[74]Dreiser, *The Stoic*,8.
[75]Dreiser, *The Stoic*,37.
[76]Dreiser, *The Stoic*,88.
[77]Dreiser, *The Stoic*,125.
[78]Dreiser, *The Stoic*,199.
[79]Dreiser, *The Stoic*,207.
[80]Dreiser, *The Stoic*,224.
[81]Dreiser, *The Stoic*,11.
[82]Dreiser, *The Stoic*,256.
[83]Dreiser, *The Stoic*,272.
[84]Dreiser, *The Stoic*,138.
[85]Dreiser, *The Stoic*,138.
[86]Dreiser, *The Stoic*,273.
[87]Dreiser, *The Stoic*,283.
[88]Dreiser, *The Stoic*,284.
[89]Dreiser, *Hey Rub-A-Dub-Dub*,86.
[90]Dreiser, *Hey Rub-A-Dub-Dub*,78-79.
[91]Dreiser, *Hey Rub-A-Dub-Dub*,81.
[92]Dreiser, *Hey Rub-A-Dub-Dub*,82.
[93]Dreiser, *The Stoic*,273.
[94]Dreiser, *The Stoic*,271.
[95]Dreiser, *The Stoic*,274.
[96]Dreiser, *Hey Rub-A-Dub-Dub*,83.

CHAPTER IV

THE "GENIUS" AND OTHER WORKS
The Novel of Power

The struggle for power and fame is the theme of the novel *The "Genius"* .The "Genius" is different from the trilogy *The Financier* , *The Titan* and the *The Stoic* in that here Dreiser does not depict craze for financial gains. Instead the hero is depicted as a man who sought beauty in art and life despite the hardship and pain which this pursuit caused himself and others.

In *The "Genius"* Dreiser undertook an autobiographical novel to justify himself as a man with artistic interest, by observing the lives and ideals of a number of young painters of his own time in particular, Shinn's New York exhibitions and Paris journey. Dreiser has incorporated his observations of artists into this novel *The "Genius"* along with his own touches of philosophy, of the futility of such an obsession which converts a Genius and master craftsman into a womanizer, a derelict and nervous wreck.

A keen observer that Dreiser was, he found enough material in his own career as an artist, reporter, magazine, writer and novelist. In the portrayal of Eugene Witla, the protagonist of the novel as a painter and director, Dreiser has delineated his own experiences as a writer and editor. There are limitations in the autobiographical element in that Dreiser is careful not to elaborate Eugene Witla's experiences as a young boy because it is not his boyhood and family background but his mature temperament and conflicts as an artist that Dreiser wishes to portray. Dreiser was quite aware that:

> A man of genius, like every other human being is limited by his environment, hence by the ideas and knowledge of

> the times; he cannot perform miracles. He can only excel, and usually in a unique and creative manner, in a function which others master to a lesser degree And the environment of it may as readily frustrate as further it.[1]

It was this very fact of frustration rather than encouragement which is Eugene Witla's lot. Both Dreiser and Eugene Witla have a successful career but their marriages are a failure because of the sensuality and conventionality of the woman to whom they are married. This is followed by a nervous breakdown and a period of struggle as a manual labourer. There is also a desire to become more and more indulgent in sex and a resultant philandering with a variety of women. The licentious artist struggles to maintain a balance between two opposing forces- his artistic temperament and his desire to escape the limitations of marriage.

Eugene's artistic temperament induces him to admire "beauty" in any form. Eugene gets fascinated by, " a soaring buzzard poised in speculative flight." or "a rose in bloom. a tree swaying in the wind ." [2]Eugene Witla, a resident of Alexandria, Illinois responds to beauty at the tender age of seventeen. So Eugene " admired girls- was mad about them- but only about those who were truly beautiful... He invested them with more beauty than they had; the beauty was in his own soul. But he did not know that."[3]

This is the beginning of all his problems in life. His instincts lead him to follow and capture beauty in the form of women and art. This instinct is at loggerheads and direct confrontation with the norms of society. Eugene is unable to restrict himself to the code of morality laid down by society and he believes that in his lady love Angela Blue he has met a perfectly compatible match. According to Donald Pfizer,

> The sense of guilt with which Dreiser portrays Eugene's sexual "overindulgence" with Angela thus has deeper roots than a conventional vampire theme in which the artist is drained off his creativity by his grosser appetites. Dreiser

was depicting as well the combination of dependence and fear, of need and anxiety, which characterized his entire sexual life and which no doubt was a major cause of his "varietistic" career.[4]

Therefore we find that the emotional attachment to women is quite strong and is cause of concern. Moreover Eugene did not believe in the sanctity of a wedding. There was no sense of commitment to his better half and this is the main cause of his ruin as "he could not face the weight and significance of the social theory that this was for life- that if he married her today, he would have to live with her all the rest of his days."[5]

This is in total contrast to Angela Blue's views of marriage. To the yellow haired cute Angela, "The utterance of the marriage vow meant just what it said, that they would cleave each to the other; there should be henceforth no thoughts, feelings or emotions and decidedly no action which would not conform with the letter and the spirit of the marriage vow."[6] This total sense of commitment of Angela Blue would naturally find disappointment in the behaviour of Eugene whose firm opinion was that:

> Marriage was a trick of nature by which you were compelled to carry out her scheme of race continuance. Love was a lure; desire a scheme of propagation devised by the way ... A child was a kind of nuisance.[7]

Eugene's nonchalance and superficial attitude to marriage with no desire to propagate his own race naturally meets with resentment from Angela. Advertising and magazine publishing help him to rise to a high position. It needs tact and a great deal of self discipline and self control; but Eugene has none of these. Instead of a single minded devotion to his vocation, his mind wavers and he begins admiring another woman Suzanne. Angela, with a wish to save her marriage becomes pregnant and Suzanne's mother, Mrs. Dale achieves her end of separating the two. Not only does he lose Suzanne but he loses his job also. Angela also dies of childbirth.

Eugene finds himself an eligible bachelor once again and returns to art. A long stream of girls Margaret Dunn , Ruby Kenny, Christina Channing, Frieda Roth, Carlotta Wilson and so on to succumb to his passion. As observed by Philip Gerber,

> Around these flames of perfect beauty Eugene flits like an excited moth, believing ever in the ultimate fulfillment of the mirage. But each happy illusion leads only to a sad disillusion. Never relinquishing entirely his fruitless search for the one girl who will be his all-in-all, Eugene moves steadily towards stoicism and the very Dreiserian admission that this is the way things are.[8]

The indiscriminate philandering with women and the incapacity to choose between art and business makes a nervous wreck of Eugene.

> Witla who had, no knowledge of the effect of one's sexual life upon one's work, not what such a life when badly arranged can do to a perfect art-how it can distort the sense of color, weaken that balanced judgement of character which is so essential to a normal interpretation of life, make all striving hopeless, take from art its most joyous conception, make life itself seem unimportant and death a relief .[9]

As it is, his wife Angela has been a termagant and his other girl friends think that he had made a mistake in marrying her. As Dreiser himself observes: "Men were more or less unstable in their make-up."[10] Eugene happens to be an embodiment of total instability that where ever he was, he flirts and this made the "Genius" in him suffer. As Donald Pfizer remarks,

> The "Genius" expresses several nineteenth century myths of the artist, with a few twentieth century cliches thrown in. The artist as Byronic or Shelleyan Hero requires freedom from social convention but must not use his freedom to fall prey to the vampire of feminine

> possessiveness. If he does fall, salvation awaits him, in his guise of Victorian Poet, through the spirituality of feminine beauty, a beauty which symbolizes Art itself...he does not betray his talent to the false goals of wealth and position.[11]

In the novel Dreiser defends Eugene's love of complete freedom and naturally, society is blamed for being too critical on Eugene. Eugene is right in following his basic instincts and it is quite rude of society to compel him to follow moral codes. An artist and for that matter a "Genius" would naturally have his eccentricities. "He liked the liberty of going where he pleased, saying nothing, not feeling it necessary to say anything. He longed for the freedom of pre-matrimonial days."[12]

So Eugene cannot be blamed for just giving vent to his natural instincts while at the same time being quite critical of his surroundings. The city of Chicago offers a delightful spectacle to the youngster Eugene.

> The vast ruck of life that had sprung suddenly into existence upon the dank marshes of a lake shore. Miles and miles of dreary little houses; miles and miles of wooden block-paved streets, with gas lamps placed and water mains laid, and empty wooden walks set for pedestrians;the beat of a hundred thousand hammers; the ring of a hundred thousand travels!. . . Engines clanging, trains moving, people watching at street crossing-pedestrians,wagon drivers, street car drivers, drays of beer, trucks of coal, brick, stone,sand a spectacle of raw, necessary life![13]

This spectacle of life revealing both poverty and gloom on the one hand and splendour, luxury and a life struggling to 'keep up with the Joneses' on the other make Eugene realise that he might have to starve if he didn't look sharp. Eugene tries to work as a day labourer and make some money. But even there he is a big failure. The artist in him would not allow him to succeed. He was upset by the dirty mud and soiled labourers and indulged in self pity that he should be one among them. He longed for his girl friend, his beautiful studio, and a luxurious artistic life. " Its seemed that life had wronged him terribly, and yet he could do nothing about it.He had no money making capacity."[14]

Eugene having formulated the theory of success to be hard work, struggles through innumerable hardships in life to reach the heights of success in New York. Having had hints of success Dreiser feels Eugene would lose the artistic spirit in him. With the improvement in status he would be able to acquire an automobile for himself and a piano for Angela but the artist in him would no longer be there. Employed by the Kalvin Publishing Co. Eugene earns quite a large sum, but this drowns the artist in him and even his way of dressing, "with a derby hat, clothes of the latest cut, a ring of oriental design on his middle finger, and pins and ties which reflected the prevailing modes," [15] indicates this change in attitude.

Monetary success does not give him the satisfaction which he is in search of. The instinctive and natural attraction to women also does not give him the psychological satisfaction which he is longing for. To him marriage is also a matter of convenience. "Certainly he would love, honour, cherish it if it were possible if not then not.[16] Eugene has his own unconventional self styled way of living and neither women nor wealth seem to offer him the happiness for which he longs. "If we are poor, wealth will seem temporarily to make us happy."[17]

If nothing gives a man with fine artistic sensibilities happiness then there is something wrong in his own mental make up. "Sunlight on the corn, colour of dawn in the maid's cheek, the moonlight on the water . . ." [18] and he could also paint life in a realistic manner "I am dirty, I am commonplace, I am grim , I am shabby, but I am life."[19]

Eugene could not understand the fact that the beauty which he was admiring in others was actually the beauty engulfed in his own soul. Ignorant of this fact he succumbs to the illusion which attracted him to beautiful girls. So powerful was the illusion of desire, "the sheer animal magnetism of beauty that when it came near him in the form of a lovely girl he could not resist it."[20] Such was the illusion in which the whole nation seemed to give into. In "Neurotic America And The Sex Impulse" Dreiser himself observes that even the churches and newspapers "preach a lofty code of ethics and morals which they themselves find difficult if not impossible to practice."[21]

Dreiser might be reminisensing his own difficulties in being faithful and devoted to his wife because he was then enamoured by Thelma Cudlipp. In the latter part of the essay "Neurotic America and the Sex Impulse" Dreiser goes on to add that:

> The truth no doubt is that in this much maligned impulse which chemical forces beyond and above the willing of men are compounding, lies the destiny of man, only we are not as yet able to fathom that destiny But one thing is certain: no hard and fast rule governing this impulse has worked with accuracy for any given length of time, any where... We hear of the duty of preserving the sanctity of the home, maintaining a wife and raising a family according to the monogamic theory..... Routine home life, even an artistic breeding-pen, can scarcely be the be-all and end-all of human existence, any more than may unrestrained license...There are those who find it confining, destroying.[22]

Therefore in the conclusive part of the same essay, Dreiser concludes saying that man would continue to generate wild fires and his passions would continue to overlap his fears and judgements and cause him to do things that may be strictly forbidden him and according to Dreiser's view, the law in all special instances is "absolutely helpless before passion.. or fix a just measure of praise or blame."[23]

Despite all these observations the fact remains that character is destiny and Eugene's character of over indulgence results in his nervous breakdown. Acclaimed by one and all to be a genius, Eugene should actually have made a success of life but is unable to do so because of certain other forces like conscience and indecision. He doesn't act when he is supposed to act. For instance in the case of tracking down Suzanne who had been abducted by her mother, he almost reaches the place where she is, but loses Suzanne because of his indecisive procrastination. "Obviously, nature had intended this as the crowning event of his life. Life recognized him as a "Genius" - the fates - it was heaping posies in his lap laying a crown of victory upon his brow."[24] Unfortunately, posies of life do not seem to reach those who do not grab them.

> The dreams of man are one thing-his Capacity to realise them another. At either poles are the accidents of supreme failure and supreme success-the supreme failure of an Abelard for instance, the supreme success of a Napoleon, enthroned at Paris.[25]

Thus Dreiser seems to impose Eugene as a character with a tragic flaw like Shakespeare's Hamlet—putting off doing things and thereby losing valuable opportunities. In dire need of some philosophical guidance, Eugene explores Christian Science. "It was his physical and mental illness which led him to consult a healer- than by the philosophical base of the faith in a concept of the spiritual nature and oneness of all existence."[26]

With all potentially great people pouring into business, Eugene does not know what is expected of him. He, who had marvelled at wealth and luxury at Chicago earlier, felt intuitively the far reaches which separate the ordinary man from the man of wealth. He had gone there with a pretty high estimate of himself but felt totally disappointed. The necessity to understand this philosophy arises when Eugene feels that,

> It was tangled life, difficult and dangerous. There was no peace in it, for there is neither peace nor happiness in deception. A burning joy was invariably followed by a disturbing remorse afterward.. We think that our actions when unseen of mortal eye resolve themselves into

> nothingness, but this is not true. They are woven indefinably into our being and shine forth ultimately as the real self, inspite of all our pretences. One could almost accept the Brahmanistic dogma of a psychic body which sees and is seen where we dream all to be darkness. There is no other supposition on which to explain the facts of intuition. So many ind'viduals have it. They know so well without knowing why they know.[27]

Angela also has this sort of an intuition in connection with Eugene. It is quite unfair for Eugene because he cannot hide nothing from her. Somehow Eugene feels disturbed because people do not value art but are readily hailing the glories and successes of businessmen. The artist in him is torn to pieces and he feels that he is not living but only existing. Life seems quite horrible and depressing.

> It was a horrible picture to him in his present condition. It was like the grinding of the millstones, upper and nether. These were the chaff. He was a part of the chaff at present or in danger of becoming so. Life was winnowing him out.[28]

Eugene Witla is highly philosophical towards the end of the novel. Having suffered a great deal throughout, Witla speculates over his own problems and over life in general. Regarding god and man as being one observes:

> Life or God is in the cell...The cell's intelligence is His. The human personality is also at last Himself and only Himself...If you wish to say 'Biologos' or God instead of life, I heartily agree...[29] So this maturity of mind offers him a balance and peace of mind. A man who was earlier torn to pieces by his own worrying nature suddenly comes to understand Dreiser's own philosophy that after all we are only atoms in this vast expanse called Universe. So instead of turning inwards and being introspective all the time if we could look out there is a great deal which

> nature can offer.Theist and Agnostic must agree in recognising the properties of space as inherent, eternal, uncreated- as anteceding all creation, if creation has taken place. Hence could we penetrate the mysteries of existence, there would still remain more transcendent mysteries.[30]

So how can man decide and criticize forms, norms and moral codes when he himself is uncertain of what nature intended to do with him. He doesn't know much about his own body 'chemism' and how they react to various situations .So it is unjustified for man to form laws and brand anyone as being amoral or immoral. All such norms are also not permanent. They are all transitory and are bound to change.

> In this huge chaotic system called life the individual came and went, acting his tiny part in the drama, stung with delight by favourable illusions, crushed by the vagaries of circumstances, and able to alter nothing in the system itself which remained as before - fixed, inscrutable, and eternal.[31]

Having resolved the crisis in his life, towards the end of the novel, Eugene Witla is seen relaxing with his daughter and observing the stars in the skies. There is an ascetic acceptance of what is in store for him. "All apparently was permitted, Eugene reflects, nothing is fixed. Perhaps life loved only change, equation, drama and laughter."[32]

Dreiser's own opinion on how to become successful in life is very clearly revealed in one of his essays "The American financier" in *Hey ,Rub-A-Dub-Dub* .In order to be successful the individual should not forget the society "Which in order to advantage himself he must flatter, satisfy or exploit..." [33] The fact remains that man has to interact with society, there is no escape from it.

In the novel *Bulwark*, published in 1946 also Dreiser elaborates on how the craze for power and wealth has corrupted the Quakers. Dreiser's mother was a Mennonite, a sect closely linked to Quakerism and she was always dressed in spotlessly clean simple clothes and had very naturalistic simple ideals in life like child bearing and rearing and had no thoughts whatsoever of any accumulation of wealth or property. Having been brought up in such a background Dreiser was naturally awe -struck to find how society was corrupting Quaker ideals of simplicity. The Quakers, the plain people surrounded "by a world where the acquisitive instinct ran riot and men madly erected temples to make money."[34]

The plight of the Quakers is that they were also attracted by this mad rush for making money. Their desires grew unsuppressible and they indulged in lavishly displaying wealth and lived a life of luxury. So *The Bulwark* is the story of the protagonist Solon Barnes' struggle to fight against the growing materialistic tendencies in his family. Actually he fails in his attempt because the world around him is more powerful than he himself -a single man.

Towards the beginning of the novel Solon Barnes' father Rufus Barnes has taught his children that God was prevalent everywhere. He believed in putting up such quotations in his children's rooms like : "He leadeth me beside the still waters; he restoreth my soul"and "In the Lord I put my trust."[35] Unfortunately something occurs to disturb their life of simplicity and peace. Rufus Barnes is approached by his widowed sister- in-law to stay in her house, repair and renovate her house and make her property, which is in ruins, attractive enough so that it becomes salable. Solon Barnes has to consent because he cannot afford to see his sister-in-law and her children suffer lack of attention and thereby ruin their lives. In entering the house Rufus finds that,

> ...For the first time in his life, he was face to face with the form if not actually the present substance, of luxury... There was... a quite ornate reception hall, a wide and handsome staircase with a carved balustrade of polished walnut...[36]

All tnese are quite disturbing to the Quaker spirit in him , but with the intention of restoring the ruined property back to his sister - in -

law he has to make a compromise, even though it proves to be too costly an affair ultimately.

Rufus, the soul of industry and honest effort sells to advantage Kimber's interest in the Trenton pottery and invests the proceeds in mortgages in the region about Trenton, and succeeds in securing for Phoebe a tidy income. He soon attains as great an esteem as his brother-in-law in the Trenton meeting. In fact, in the course of the ten years which elapse between his arrival and his son's marriage to Benecia Wallin, the material and social aspects of the Barnes' family changes considerably. So the family's rise socially and materially meant to Hannah Barnes, Rufus' wife a loss of "pristine simplicity and humility which all friends valued so highly she wished they might be made to see that great wealth might readily prove a genuine spiritual handicap." [37]

This fear of wealth and prosperity was so strong in Hannah that she dreamt of some possible ruin to her son's spiritual faith and belief. Hannah Barnes dreamt one day that while her son Solon leapt astride a handsome black mare, it revolted and later on while he was about to "break the mare to his will" and ride comfortably it rushed forward, hit a fence and threw him down.

> What could it mean? And although she decided to say nothing to anyone, there was the feeling that in some way or other it might be connected with this visit with the Wallins to Oakwold. Or, if not that, then with the sudden shift in their material and social status.[38]

According to Philip Gerber the interpretation of this scene is as follows:

> The dream foreshadows Solon's struggle to tame the materialistic forces rampant in the world, to subordinate them and sensuality to the religious will. But instead the mare of the world at last throws him and disastrously.[39]

The mare of the world not only throws Solon down but

it also throws his five offspring down. Even though Solon inculcates Quakerism in their minds right from their tenderest years it so happens that as they grow up, they allow themselves to succumb to the pressures of the outside world. They have some inborn innate urges or "chemisms" which happen to be their guiding spirits as they bloom. The preachings at home are outdone by the pressures of society. All the "spiritual unworldliness"[40] of their homes are insignificant in the face of this vast and expansive social world. Dreiser wrote to Upton Sinclair in 1924, "that the brotherhood of man...is mere moonshine to me. I see the individual large or small ,weak or strong as predatory and nothing else."[41]

In *Bulwark* also Solon's children follow their own course unmindful of their father's preachings. Solon's daughter Isobel remains a withdrawn and isolated girl because she is not quite attractive and unable to lure suitors. Dorothea who happens to be a beautiful daughter has dreams of escaping from her quiet Thornborough home to the dazzling world of jewels and clothes. It so happens that Solon's youngest daughter Etta has an artistic turn of mind, and has a dreamy adventurous spirit and explores places away from home along with her friend Volida on whom she develops a "crush".None of them are worried about their parents or are conscious of the fact that they should cling to one another and remain as a close knit family.

The sons are no better. Orville is quite frugal and miserly ,while Stewart is only concerned with physical pleasures and a life of variety and colour. So none of the children stick to Quakerism and a simple austere life. Orville actually longs to live a luxurious life with a beautiful home, gardens, servants, carriages and horses.

All this proves that Hannah Barnes' dream is correct after all. All of them stay away from the code of conduct of Quakers. Isobel succumbs to her own miseries because she is unable to accommodate and balance her Quaker Principles with those of college life which according to her was actually converting girls into snobs. On the other hand Etta is rather innocent and of a romantic spirit that she is ready to destroy herself by remaining the mistress of a painter. Solon is unable to understand the mystery of it all. He questions religion and tries to analyse the reason why religion fails to offer a solution to his problem,and he is surprised "that inspite of a divinely ordered scheme of things and a willingness on the manifested plan, as far as one could determine it, still these things would occur."[42]

The tragic end of Stewart's dissolute life is most disturbing. The pleasure seeking romantic youngster who resorts to stealing from his aunt first and then his mother too in order to chauffeur rich young girls on outings, is ultimately put behind bars for having accidentally drugged one of the girls to death. Unable to digest this drastic insult, Stewart commits suicide in jail.

The Bulwark is thus a story of a Quaker who is undetterred in his religious faith, even though his children are being influenced and corrupted by a so called modern outlook. Dreiser's attitude towards religion as being all humbug is clearly indicated in this novel. All basic natural instincts like possessing a beautiful house, a pretty wife, powerful friends and good health is there in almost all human beings. Then why should religion suppress such instincts, was what troubled Dreiser.

Once when Solon moved about the city he got a glimpse of true, city life. The sights were definitely painful to him. There were:

> Large neighbourhoods crowded with the exceedingly poor; houses of prostitution openly and flagrantly conducted; Saloons and dives elbowing each other at street corners and patronised by the shabbiest and most forlorn of human derelicts.[43]

The irony of the situation is not in this observation but in the fact that Solon's father had taught him to "avoid any contact with them, " and "to take a firm hold on the religious life in order to escape the miseries of a godless one."[44]

As a preacher shouldn't he have taken more interest in improving the lot of such downtrodden, underprivileged people rather than accepting it as God's will and isolating himself from direct interaction with such unfortunate people? All this shamming and hypocrisy in religionists was what was denounced by Dreiser.

Solon himself observes toward the close of the novel when Stewart is no more: "This wretched world, with its temptations and unbridled pleasures, had done this to his son, had lured his son and Etta from him -and that inspite of all he had tried to do or say."[45] So none of his sayings or doings had any positive effect on his family. His colleague's observations of Solon's weakness is: "The only trouble with his principles is that they're too high for these days . . . ."[46]

So the fact remains that as long as there is evil in society, man's innate chemisms will continue attracting countless numbers into its vile net. By the last quarter of the nineteenth century the Quakers were also becoming quite modern and their faith was being suppressed by money -mindedness. So even in Solon's character we find that he represents "the bulwark of sound business sense"[47], and his success as a director of the Traders and Builders Bank of Philadelphia is almost as resounding as his success in the meeting house. Indeed Solon cannot separate the two activities. Success in life, is to him simply the adjunct of goodness. In Solon's mind therefore the operations of the banks and the laws of commerce are directly connected with Divine Will,and the control of money is a kind of stewardship under God.

Actually Dreiser was able to find a parallel between the activities of the Quakers with those of communists. Both were insisting on the fact that if man is to lead a better quality of life then the profit motive should be dispensed with. As far as religionists are concerned, Dreiser was of the opinion that they were trying to make him conform to some conventionality or other which he was actually determined to do away with. "As for taboos, or rules of organised society, they are most often for the dumb, and one need scarcely trouble as to those. They will remain dumb and useless."[48]

A poem of Dreiser's "what to do ?" which was published in 1945 helps us view his theory and outlook on life very clearly:

> In the meantime one
> A small -town editor writes the truth
> about profit and starvation . . .
> And one, the educator, says to the child,
> A.B.C and to the adult, Learn !
> Know that the world grows smaller!
> And one, the minister, says to all,
> love thy neighbour as thyself.
> And one, the lover of his fellow man says
> Take, from each according to his ability;
> Give to each according to his need.[49]

The last statement gives Dreiser's views on how to make the world a better place to live in. Theodore Dreiser's theory that life is here and now and should be enjoyed to the full at this very instant. In a short story, "Chains" Dreiser observes:

> Beauty, beauty, beauty! How could one gainsay the charm or avoid the lure of it? Not he, for one. Trig, beautiful women, who carried themselves with an air and swing and suggested by their every movement passion, alertness, gaiety of mind! The church bells might ring and millions of religionists preach of a life hereafter with a fixed table of rewards and punishments, but what did anyone know of the future, anyhow? Nothing ! exactly nothing inspite of all the churches.Life appeared and disappeared again; ...here and now was life, here and now beauty...[50]

All these are the observations of the protagonist who is in the clutches of a wastrel and who sticks to admiring her even though he knew that he was not the only man in her life. Ultimately anyhow he makes his escape.

While presenting realistic accounts of the multifarious urges of human beings, Dreiser is quite sensitive to the fact that not all urges are for something good or better. Not all change is for the better. In a short story "Free", Rufus Haymaker the protagonist is calm and composed and waiting for his wife to die. He imagines that he had not been happy with her all along and that once she dies, he would be a free man once again -he would become an eligible suitor.

Haymaker is of the opinion that he had not actually lived life till then, he had only been drifting and that he should have ended his marriage even earlier. So anxiously he awaits his freedom. It is not all that easy to get one's freedom after all. Here the questions of morals also arise and he wonders: "Was there not some psychic law governing this matter of union -one life, one love - which made the thoughts and the pains and the subsequent sufferings and hardships of the individual, whatever they might be, seem unimportant? The churches said so."[52]

The preachings of the church and societal norms do make him change his opinion and he wonders whether he had not been at fault for having wished that his wife should die. His mind reconciles itself to the fact that :

> She had tried hadn't she ? - only she had not been able to make a success of things, as he saw it , and he had not been able to love her, that was all. He reproached himself once more now with the hardness and the cruelty of his thoughts. [53]

Ultimately after her death Mr. Haymaker wonders as to what was the benefit after all. His skin was wrinkled, there were crow's -feet at the sides of his eyes and what was once a striking, forceful, dynamic body is now transformed into an unattractive and ungainly one because of his old age. There is pathos in the observation which Mr. Haymaker makes at the close of the story, "Free. I know now how that is. I am free now, at last !Free! ...Free! ...Yes -Free... to die!"[54]

Comparing the two short stories it is found that neither the protagonist of "Chains" nor the protagonist of "Free" is happy and for different reasons. If the first one longs for escape from a prostitute the second one wants to be freed from his institutionalized marriage to an industrious, frugal and beautiful woman. So either way man is not ready to accept marriage as a "sacrament, sacrosanct, never to be dissolved. One life, one love. Once a man had accepted the yoke or even asked a girl to marry him it was his duty to abide by it."[55] This was indeed a difficult ordeal! To Dreiser it was very difficult to stick to conventional ideas and opinions.

To him woman was always a witch or a troll of whom he could never be sure. He liked reading his own inconsistencies into women of his choice and could more easily forgive erratic conduct than a boring conformity to convention, as he saw it, or a restraining hand upon himself. [56]

In "The Old Neighbourhood' a story from his collection in Chains the protagonist is quite a poor man. "He was crazy for success, wild with a desire for a superior, contemptuous position in the world."[57] This craziness brings about his downfall as wealth and avarice cannot bring happiness. Ultimately he realises that "here is something cruel and evil in it all, in all wealth, all ambition, in love of fame -too cruel."[58]

In another short story "Fulfillment" the heroine "Ulrica" happens to fall in love with an artist after many flirtations with many eligible young men. She had rejected all her earlier suitors because they tried to lure her with their wealth and had neither imagination nor intelligence. With Vivian things were different. Vivian had an artistic bent of mind and it is she who manages the show by working as a stage artist. Here also as in all Dreiser's works Vivian "...seemed to need her as much as she needed him, to yearn with an intense hunger over her as a thing of beauty -he who to her was strength, beauty, ideals, power, all the substance of beauty and delight that she could crave."[59]

Their life seems to be quite harmonious and beautiful and they actually imagine themselves to be in paradise. Unfortunately Vivian dies of influenza dashing all their hopes. Then comes Ulrica's disinterested marriage of convenience with a businessman of fifty. Harry, a dejected lover needs Ulrica's company and in return takes care of her and her mother. Fame, money and friendship are all hers and Harry brings about a fulfillment of all her unrealised hopes. "Both Harry and Ulrica are depressed, unfulfilled lovers seeking to rectify life's deprivations in their newly found relationship."[60]

Ulrica's earlier flirtations were all biological necessities but her ultimate choice is a psychological acceptance or resignation in order to fulfill her unfulfilled commitments to her sole lover Vivian. Instead of an idealistic view of life where she should have had to remain single, Ulrica chose a realistic view of life with an intention of achieving her ends.

Thus all men whether strong or weak are all acted upon by chemisms or driving forces. The strong men proceed with satiating their urges whereas the weak who are depicted as being conventional thinking and who are religious too are unable to assimilate the fact that biological urges are powerful and can sometimes ruin too. They are unable to accept any thing which according to them is amoral or immoral even though it may be biologically true. At this Dreiser says, I often ask my self why do not the argued morals of the world prevail if they are so important, or if the immorality of the world is so destructive and plague like, why has it not destroyed the world ? Why the ever lasting contest between them, the everlasting palaver as to their sinfulness? Is it not obvious that both are essential and that equation which we know as life is thus struck between them?[61]

Even in his poems Dreiser tries to reform social injustice. In a poem entitled "Reformer" Dreiser observes :

I tried to help men
Contemplating with pain
The fallen,
The tortured,
The hopeless ,
I spoke for them,
Wrote to them,
Formed a band
That sought to change by force
Or opposition
The creed.
And Vanity of others
. . . .

But despite all his attempts at reforming society, he finds that society ensures that it imprisons and punishes him for his audacious attempt to reform it.

Seeking to help,
I was marked
And later,
Seized by men of power
. . . . . .
I was denounced
Imprisoned
Laughed at
Despised
For my dreams.[62]

Observing such a state of affairs where one can not dream what one wishes to dream, it is no wonder, that for sometime Dreiser took to communism, where one is taught what to dream, as a panacea for all ills. In *Hoosier Holiday* he observes - " Dream on Believe. Perhaps it is unwise, foolish, child like, but dream anyhow," for, of dreams and the memory of them is life compounded."[63]

For after all man has to live, and live successfully, so unless he dreams and plans how can he succeed? In *A traveller at forty* Dreiser gives an account of his travels in Europe. There, in that book Dreiser accepts the fact that he is not sure of many things:

> For myself I accept now no creeds. I do not know what truth is, what beauty is, what love is, what hope is. I do not believe anyone absolutely. I think people are both evil and well intentioned.[64]

So there are no absolutes in life. Everything is bound to change. If at times life is a grim battle for survival at other times it is generous and lovable, beautiful. When the poor suffer and the rich are well provided for, one tends to feel that there is lack of justice in this universe. Other times Dreiser felt: " I have always felt, inspite of all my cravings, that somehow in a large way there is a rude justice done under the sun, and that a balance for, I will not say right, but for happiness is maintained."[65]

So life is a mixture of opposites and therefore spicier, more relishable. If all human beings were alike then there would be monotony. The one thing Dreiser is quite sure about is that man should work hard and succeed and not just while away his time. Dreiser in his heart of hearts hates the offspring of wealthy men who keep rollicking in wealth earned without labour.

> I refuse to think that it is either necessary or inevitable that I, or any other man, should work for a few dollars a day, skimping and longing, while another, a dunce, who never did anything but... should take the heavy profits of my work and stuff them into his pockets.[66]

In *Tragic America* also Dreiser strongly objects to the same phenomenon - "One girl, for instance, with eight hundred million dollars, amuses herself as best she may, while another slaves for six or eight dollars a week."[67] As wealth was becoming a family affair Dreiser wished that there should be equal opportunity for all. Here also Dreiser found that: "The cunning and the strong have made great use of the land of real opportunity ."[68]

It so happened that these opportunists or industrialists as they were called were in actuality the law makers too. Dreiser felt that the Government could not take one step without the approval of a John D.Rockefeller, Jr., Walter Teagle, a Charles Schwab, an Owen D.Young, a William Loeb, a Walter S.Gifford, or their employees and superiors. He also felt that it was these men and not the Government which actually ruled. One of them actually told Dreiser blandly: "Who's to stop us?" [69]

Its no wonder that capitalism became a failure, as the common man was to be seen nowhere in the picture. It was with an intention of pointing such injustice that Dreiser has written novels such as *The Financier* , *The Stoic* or *The Titan* . "America is today not only the richest nation in the world; it has the greatest inequality of wealth and the most centralized ownership and control in the history of the race..."[70] This was the observation made by John H. Gray, Head of Dept. of economics, Graduate school of the American University. Dreiser has himself observed in an essay entitled "Some Aspects of our National Character" in *Hey Rub-A-Dub-Dub* that even though men are created equal, " the curious fact remains that the strong, the ruthless, the shrewd get along as well here as they do anywhere and that they are constantly developing ways and foreshortening his peace and happiness in favour of their own."[71]

The sympathy with the labour class is replete in Dreiser's works. In another essay entitled "The Toil of the Labourer" in *Hey,Rub-A-Dub-Dub*, Dreiser observes that the toilers or labourers who did not have the calibre to do anything better were being treated quite indifferently by Nature. "It was little to her whether they lived or died, did poorly or well."[72]

The fact also remained that in case these workers did not toil then there could be only "death" and "disintegration" awaiting them. They had to bear with the "rough" and "exacting" (P. 102) attitude of their masters and continue labouring. In case these labourers or grocers or plumbers wished to improve their position then they should start using their brains to devise the means of improving. It is here that they fall short. "It seems to me that the average cat reasons quite as well as the average plumber or grocer, if not better." [73]

The culprits are the theories and "isms" with which we are habituated. Dreiser refers to his father's pagan attitudes and religiosity and criticizes him saying that he had done all this with a view of getting a place with the fairies and elves in Christendom. So all social values and cultures, all our conventions and beliefs are difficult to break and therein lies the problem. Once a man is able to free himself of all this and live with a broad open mind, then life would definitely change for the better.

So we find that the first few novels *Sister Carrie* and *Jennie Gerhardt* speak of man's struggle to rise out of poverty and make an ex1stence in this work. The next set of novels, the trilogy *The Financier* , *The Titan* and *The Stoic* deal with the financial wizards in society whose main aim is to stride upon the weak and rise as high as possible.

The "Genius" and other short stories point out how man is guided by his chemisms to such an extent that society is unable to accept it as moral and therefore they are ruined. *The Bulwark* on the other hand astounds the readers by revealing the fact that religious people like Quakers who lead a simple life are ruined as soon as they dream of living a life of sophistication and luxury.Even business dealings in banks are not for the religious minded Solon. His associates deceive him swindling large sums and depositing it in "Shaky concerns controlled by themselves"[74] Solon has no other way out but to resign and lose his job while preserving his religion.

No one can state very clearly whether some thing is right or wrong and the man made laws are also not very clear about it .So if *The Titan* is successfully swindling money and becoming powerful, Solon of *The Bulwark* is successfully upholding the Quaker policies of simplicity and honesty. Also there is no poetic justice as in Shakespeare that evil shall be punished and good rewarded. No, sometimes it happens to be reverse evil men get rewarded as in *The Financier* and *The Titan* with wealth and power, while, the honest Quaker suffers to see his children getting corrupted one after the other in *The Bulwark*.

While considering the possibility of Communism to offer a solution to the injustice meted out to common labourers in America, he was at the same time wide awake to the filth, squalor and dirt found all over in Russia, raptured by the social order in Russia, he observes, "This is Russia... This is the new, shifting, shimmering, changeful, colourful, classless day of a new social order. A new world indeed ."Dreiser is at the same time aware of its flaws too :-

> You live too many in one room and are lunatic enough to identify it with a communistic spirit. I rise to complain. And I suggest in this connection that more Individualism and less communism would be to the great advantage of this mighty country. [75]

So the wide awake realist is deeply observant, sensitive and gives a very factual and truthful representation of his ideas and beliefs in his works. In a poem entitled "Life" in his collection of poems *Moods* Dreiser observes :-

> It is so beautiful
> Its very end with a strange beauty blends
> Into a sweeter, richer harmony
> . . . .
> Who would be happy and there was no
> pain.[76]

Man has to suffer to realise what is happiness. If there is no suffering then how is man to know how much he has struggled to achieve whatever he has achieved. Pain and pleasure are intermingled, inseparable aspects of life.

NOTES AND REFERENCES

[1]Dreiser, "The Problem of Genius" from *Notes on Life*,177-178.

[2]Dreiser. *The "Genius"* (New York: John Lane & Co.),11-12.

[3]Dreiser. *The "Genius"*,15.

[4]Pfizer, *The Novels of Theodore Dreiser*,141.

[5]Dreiser, *The "Genius"*,190.

[6]Dreiser, *The "Genius"*,210.

[7]Dreiser, *The "Genius"*,191.

[8]Gerber, *Theodore Dreiser Revisited*,68.

[9]Dreiser, *The "Genius"*,246.

[10]Dreiser, *The "Genius"*,211.

[11]Pfizer, *The Novels of Theodore Dreiser*,142.

[12]Dreiser, *The "Genius"*,252.

[13]Dreiser, *The "Genius"*,37.

[14]Dreiser, *The "Genius"*,390.

[15]Dreiser, *The "Genius"*,433.

[16]Dreiser, *The "Genius"*,191.

[17]Dreiser, *The "Genius"*,195.

[18]Dreiser, *The "Genius"*,216.

[19]Dreiser, *The "Genius"*,222.

[20]Dreiser, *The "Genius"*, 264.

[21]Dreiser, *Tragic America* (New York: H. Liveright. 1931),126.

[22]Dreiser, *Tragic America*,136-137.

[23]Dreiser, *Tragic America*,140.

[24]Dreiser, *The "Genius"*,654.

[25]Dreiser, *The "Genius"*,711.

[26]Pfizer, *The Novels of Theodore Dreiser*,149.

[27]Dreiser, *The "Genius"*,353.

[28]Dreiser, *The "Genius"*,307-308.

[29]Dreiser, *The "Genius"*,677.

[30]Dreiser, *The "Genius"*,715.

[31]Gerber, *Theodore Dreiser Revisited*,74.

[32]Dreiser, *The "Genius"*,726.

[33]Dreiser, "The American Financier" in *Hey Rub-A-Dub-Dub*, 74-91.

[34]Gerber, *Theodore Dreiser Revisited*, 96.

[35]Dreiser, *The Bulwark*,26.

[36]Dreiser, *The Bulwark*, 11.

[37]Dreiser, *The Bulwark*,60.

[38]Dreiser, *The Bulwark*,61- 62.

[39]Gerber, *Theodore Dreiser Revisited*,109.

[40]Dreiser, *The Bulwark*,91.

[41]Dreiser to Sinclair, Dec.18,1924; Lilly Indiana University

[42]Dreiser, *TheBulwark*, 127.

[43]Dreiser, *TheBulwark*,93.

[44]Dreiser, *TheBulwark*,93.

[45]Dreiser, *TheBulwark*,297.

[46]Dreiser, *TheBulwark*,305.

[47]Pfizer, *Novels of Theodore Dreiser*,329.

[48]Dreiser , *A Book About Myself*(New York: World Publishing Co., 1965),587.

[49] Dreiser,"What to do?" Free World IX (March 1945),10.

[50]Dreiser, *Chains (*New York: Boni & Liveright, 1927),78.

[51]Dreiser, *Best Short Stories of Theodore Dreiser* Ed- James T. Farrell (Greenwich. Conn.:Fawcett.1956),41.

[52]Dreiser, *Best Short Stories of Theodore Dreiser*,50.

[53]Dreiser, *Best Short Stories of Theodore Dreiser*, ,61

[54]Dreiser, *Best Short Stories of Theodore Dreiser*, 68.

[55]Dreiser, *Best Short Stories of Theodore Dreiser*, 46.

[56]Tjader, *Dreiser:A New Dimension*, 79-80.

[57]Dreiser, *Chains*,228.

[58]Dreiser, *Chains*,247.

[59] Dreiser, *Fulfillment and other Tales of Women & Men* (Santa Rosa: Black Sparrow Press, 1992), 160.

[60]Dreiser, *Fulfillment and other Tales of Women*, 166.

[61]Florence Leaver. *"Theodore Dreiser: Beyond Naturalism"*Marktwain Quarterly,9 (1951-54), 5-9.

[62]Dreiser, *Moods*, (New York: Simon and Schuster 1935),166-67.

[63]Dreiser, *A Hoosier Holiday(*New York: John Lane, 1916), 512-513.

[64]Dreiser, *A Traveller at Forty*(New York: Century, 1913),4.

[65]Dreiser, *A Traveller at Forty*, 162.

[66]Dreiser, *A Hoosier Holiday,*181.

[67]Dreiser, *Tragic America,*6-7.

[68]Dreiser, *Tragic America,*7.

[69]Dreiser, *Tragic America,*68.

[70]Dreiser, *Tragic America,*425.

[71]Dreiser, *Hey Rub-A-Dub-Dub,*44.

[72]Dreiser, *Hey Rub-A-Dub-Dub,*96.

[73]Dreiser, *Hey Rub-A-Dub-Dub,*111.

[74]Gerber, *Theodore Dreiser Revisited,*103.

[75]Dreiser, "To The Russian People" (January, 13, 1928) Transcript (CU).

[76]Dreiser, *Moods* (New York, 1935),420.

CHAPTER V

An American Tragedy
The Role of Social and Biological Determinisms

Theodore Dreiser, the champion of the underdog was unhappy at the fast pace at which the Americans were moving. There was a mad rush for "Success", no matter what spiritual and moral codes men had to transgress in order to achieve it.While describing the American scene in *Tragic America* Dreiser has pointed out how there is immense activity all around him but people were unaware of where the hustle bustle were to lead them. There were more and more machinery ,the cars were faster ,the skyscrapers were becoming taller and the cities according to him were becoming larger such that,

> The average individual today is really tortured; he is so numerous, so meaningless, so wholly confused and defeated. In short, the general condition of the industrial life of our great cities and towns is enough to destroy the nervesas well as the comfort of many sensitive persons, in some instances driving them to suicide.[1]

Theodore Dreiser had read similar newspaper article of at least three men Carlyle Harris (in 1893), Chester Gillette (in 1906) and Clarence Richesen (in 1911). A man had fallen in love with a poor woman but with the desire of succeeding in life, had won the favour of a rich girl. At this instant the poor girl announcing her pregnancy threatened to ruin him if she was not accepted. In a state of desperation the man murdered her and faced trial. This was the same story in all the three instances. Dreiser was agonised to find how the American Dream of success was ruining the lives of many a young man.

This is the exact condition described in *An American Tragedy* also. The grappling for money and success in life, the struggle to improve one's social status, no matter whatever the cost is what brings about excessive disaster in the lives of people. The world is comparable to a vast jungle, with everyone moving according to their urges and slowly graduating from a state of absolute innocence, to an awareness that there is a great deal of evil also in society.

The hero of the novel *An American Tragedy* by Theodore Dreiser is Clyde Griffiths. Clyde's behaviour and attitude towards society even as a young boy helps us to believe, that having fallen prey to social attraction and so called luxuries of life, Clyde was moving in the direction of destruction.

In his ideographic Plan For *An American Tragedy* Dreiser has himself explained (in a letter to Harrison smith)[2] that his novel was to set forth in three distinct, social, as well as economic phases, and explain the career of a very sensitive yet not very highly mentally equipped boy. In the opening phase the boy's life is painfully hampered by poverty and a low social state from which, he seeks to extricate himself. For him love and material comfort, as well as a foolish dream of social superiority are the motivating forces.

Part One of his book is devoted to setting forth such social miseries which depress, inhibit and frustrate, and therefore exaggerate, the emotions and desires of a very sensitive boy poorly equipped for the great life struggle which confront all youth.

Part Two particularly shows how such a temperament might face a much more fortunate world which would intensify all his deepest desires for luxury and love, and how poverty and ignorance and desire engulfs him and he finds himself defeated and even charged with murder, as is the case of Griffiths in the book.

Part Three of the book shows how such an inhibited, weak temperament, once in the hands of his dreams and later the law, is forced by an ignorant, conventional and revengeful background of men who by reason of their lack of social and religious inhibitions and beliefs, do not understand his condition and so judge him quite harshly.

So in the third stage of his development Dreiser felt that the individual is not wholly responsible for social evils; it is the society which is responsible as a whole and only if society changes can there be an eradication of the ills of society. In *An American Tragedy* the whole society is projected as if it is a vast jungle and the individual is attacked from all sides by dreams of success in life, of hobnobbing with the elite in society, of going out with and being acknowledged by well known social circles. With so many pressures all around him a man can very well be expected to make wrong calculations and be totally blamed for it. This is what has been termed by "Charles Child Walcutt" in his "Theodore Dreiser and the Divided stream" as mechanistic determinism.

Man begins to act in a predetermined manner in a given situation. But the fact remains that the end results are different because those who are stinking rich can afford to have justice on their sides where as those whose pockets are empty, have to face the "chair" as Clyde does.

Clyde Griffiths is quite a normal, healthy boy of twelve who is quite averse to his parents' preachings in the streets. Also he is quite proud and ambitious and cannot imagine being tied down to a life of simplicity and poverty forever. Moreover even at the outset of *An American Tragedy* it is quite clear that the children are brought up in an impracticably moralistic manner with no knowledge of worldly affairs.

> For Clyde's parents had proved impractical in the matter of the future of the children. They did not understand the importance or the essential necessity for some form of practical or professional training for each and everyone of their young ones... they had neglected to keep their children in school in any one place... they were quite

poor and could not go to school.[3]

In such a family background, it is no wonder that once unleashed the children run amuck and go astray. Clyde is bit by the bug of American dream of success and secures a job as an assistant to a soda water clerk. Later on he becomes a bell boy at one of the prestigious hotels -"Green Davidson",, and he is rather taken aback by the vast change between the Puritanic life at home and life at the hotel. Clyde also dreams of becoming a "man about town" or "a man of wealth"(p.48) Clyde is convinced "that the chief business of life for any one with a little money or social position was to attend a theatre, a ball -game in season, or to dance, motor, entertain friends at dinner, or to travel to New York, Europe, Chicago. California."[4]

Misguided notions of life wherein money and sex dominate are what impress Clyde at the hotel. With such a basic knowledge of life Clyde proceeds to face life alone on his own when he runs away from his hometown after the automobile accident, killing a child.

In Book Two, Clyde secures a job in a Collar factory owned by his uncle Sammuel Griffiths. Life is not easy for him at the factory because of the disparity in positions between his uncle and himself. Neither his cousins, nor the employees in the factory, nor the social world is able to accept him as Sammuel Griffith's nephew. Everyone treats him as an inferior relative of Sammuel Griffiths. This anomalous position of being treated as a worker while his uncle was the owner gnaws him and he is unable to accept it.

In order to seek respite from his agony, he enters into a clandestine affair with one of his women employees, Roberta. Ironically while Clyde is in love with Roberta, Roberta dreams of life and youth and the pleasures associated with it; little does she know that all these would be short lived.All these innocent fantasies of life are ruined because of the fact that she was not born rich. On the other hand there is the other girl in Clyde's life by whom he is attracted just because she has a "...Lovely face, smart clothes, gay and superior demeanour."[5]

So much for Clyde's naturalistic temperament. He always dreams of having more and more money and also to be able to dress in the Gilbert Griffiths fashion and to ride around in one of the handsome cars he sported. Sondra Finchley the embodiment of both beauty and money is naturally a stronger and more magnetic an attraction than Roberta, that Clyde is very ready to give up his first love with whom he had grown so close to have had physical relationships also, for her sake. So much for the effect of wealth, beauty, "the peculiar social state to which he most aspired, on a temperament that was a fluid and unstable as water."[6]

So the tragedy is one of malignity motivated by the social impulses, trends and dreams of that period -the dream of accumulating more wealth and possessing women of exquisite beauty who could associate themselves with the elite in society. Harnessed by such notions which were quite prevalent in society, one is not totally astonished to find Clyde behaving in the way he does, plotting the murder of Roberta when he finds that she is pregnant. Having made some unsuccessful attempts to abort the child, Clyde wishes to get rid of her so that he could lead a more materially successful life with Sondra Finchley. Clyde's is not an occasional incident, because the lawyer who pleads on Clyde's behalf Belknap also explains how he had also had an affair with one girl, who got pregnant, and how he had sent her away and married another. The difference between the two of them is that Belknap had wealthy parents and so they helped him have his way whereas Clyde's parents were so poor that they were unable to support their own family even, and so Clyde had to face ultimate ruin.

Clyde actually becomes a victim of chance because even though he had ambitious plans and had thought of clearing out Roberta from being a hindrance in his way. The final death which comes as a blow to one and all occurs accidently. According to Philip Gerber:-

Clyde is temperamentally unfit to perpetrate the deed

> in cold blood. The extended scenes preliminary to the drowning of Roberta are prolonged by Clyde's vacillation,his nervous bungling. his decision and indecision... stalling, searching for time, deciding and reconsidering. Clyde wanders with Roberta from lake to lake, ostensibly searching for the ideal Honeymoon spot,but actually seeking the seclusion appropriate to a bloody deed and the courage to kill.[7]

Here Dreiser very dramatically depicts what the American Dream can do to a man ; how the dream impinges on every act of his and makes him appear like a professional murderer. The psychological turmoil which he undergoes depicts clearly the fact that Clyde's dream of success is like a monster,a leviathan ready to swallow him whole and finish him off. What happens to Clyde could happen to any American of his temperament and the fact that he vacillates and procrastinates proves that he has an awakened conscience. Unfortunately Clyde's lack of awareness of the fact that his soul's yearning for wealth, which is by itself perishable, can make him perish along with it and lead him to his destruction.

The ambiguity of the situation is whether he is or is not guilty of causing her accidental death. Roberta was accidentally struck by Clyde' s camera and having fallen into the water, drowned. Clyde deliberately avoids rushing to her rescue while she screams for help, afraid that he might also be dragged to death; or partly because he is still inclined to get rid of her. This scene is ironically a total violation of the calm, serene atmosphere where in Clyde patiently awaits his first encounter with Roberta.

> The air was laden with spices. . . the mingled fragrance of many grasses and flowers. There was a light wind stirring ...there were stars ...He stood listening, dreaming and watching, the rustling corn behind him stirring an old recollection in him.[8]

Clyde actually compares Roberta with his older flames and is quite pleased to note that she was more pleasant and was not calculating or indiscriminate like his older friends. Clyde is fascinated by such outward attractions as "a better collar, a nicer shirt, finer shoes, a good suit," all trappings of a materialistic society. Roberta is quite simple and caring and sends money to her aged parents. Clyde does not help his parents in such a manner. Clyde seems to be a self-centered, youth who philanders indiscriminatingly and is not quite serious about any relationship except for the social status it affords.

It is rather unfortunate that Roberta has to suffer the pangs of an unwanted pregnancy just because of her poverty and the fact that she does not have any connections with the elite in society. No doctor is ready to help her, whereas if the same condition had occurred to another girl, a daughter of socially responsible parents, the situation would have been different. As Dr.Glenn, the doctor whom Roberta approaches reminiscences:-

> He had assisted in extricating from the consequences of their folly several young girls of good family who had fallen from grace and could not otherwise be rescued, still he was opposed to aiding either by his own countenance or skill,any lapses or tangles "not heavily sponsored by others", and to help Roberta would be "too dangerous and ethically and socially wrong and criminal in the bargain."[9]

Here it is clear that Dreiser is not at all happy with society with its dual policies - one for the underdog and another for the privileged. The novel is thus a novel of social injustice. Unlike a Greek or Miltonic hero who falls from "a high estate", Dreiser's Clyde is a commoner who is left to face injustice in society. At the end of the novel we are not tempted to feel that the wicked have been punished and justice has prevailed, instead we are aroused to acknowledge an unjust, amoral society which has different yardsticks for judging different people and that Clyde's life has been ruined unnecessarily. Dreiser has himself acknowledged that he wanted the reader to see for himself - "The determining social and economic forces surrounding the individuals of all classes and within which they move to their comfort and destruction."[10]

The height of the pathos is when at the end of the novel Clyde's mother understands that there was an abysmal lack of communication between her and Clyde -she had failed in her duty as a mother. Indirectly she is also responsible for his fate -

> It is as though there was an unsurmountable wall or impenetrable barrier between them, built by the lack of understanding -for it was just that. She would never understand his craving for ease and luxury, for beauty, for love, his particular kind of love that went with show, pleasure, wealth, position, his eager and immutable aspirations and desires. She could not understand these things. She would look on all of it as sin -evil, selfishness.[11]

The judgement, the enquiry into his whereabouts on the eventful day of Roberta's death, the publication of Roberta's letters -all these are politically motivated. Orville Mason and Hon. Alvin Belknap are both contestants for the post of country judge. Both wish to impress the public with their versions of Clyde's story so that they could ultimately win the public vote and emerge winners themselves. While Mason wishes to speed up the process of prosecution before elections, Belknap wishes to delay it so that once prolonged he might emerge as winner as not to allow Mason to sway public opinion in his favour. For this reason Belknap is even ready to replace Clyde's own version with something else by concocting some other story -the actual one changed or modified in some way which would make it appear less cruel or legally murderous.

What sort of justice could be expected in such a situation? All moves are unfair, politically motivated and concocted from which no justice can virtually emerge. All characters are plotting in different manners to achieve their personal ends be it a justice or even a commoner like Clyde. All of them are chasing false values cherished and reversed by society. None seem to be morally determined to uphold the truth.

Dreiser expects us to judge Clyde's failure as a failure of

the values of the social system to which he belonged. Clyde was a man who dreamt of marrying Sondra Finchley so that he could enjoy the accompaniments of such a wedding :-" One would have a cook and servants, a great house and car,no one to work for, and only orders to give."[12]

It was such a dream which was nurtured by society. He was not the only one to have dreamt so. Many Americans had fallen prey to it. It is but natural that the upsetting of such a dream would have consequences to follow. The unwanted pregnancy of Roberta which stands to ruin his prospects in life leads Clyde to ruminate on murder. This situation would not have occurred if Clyde had not been influenced by impermanent values and standards set by society to be lured by prospects of wealth, power and assurance. So in a sense, society with its inverted values is to blame for his failure.

The worst flaw or a tragic flaw in Clyde's character is that he is unable to think coherently and act without confusion. Society has influenced him with ideas of philandering with rich girls and gaining material wealth. In his own life he should have been able to act boldly and be less of a moralistic coward. There is some truth when Belknap argues that it was not craftiness but cowardice which led him to run away from the scene as soon as he found Roberta drowned. It was also cowardice once again which prevented him from marrying Roberta; he was afraid of losing his job at his uncle's factory. It was a rule in that factory that the supervisors should not have anything to do with the girls working in the factory. Strictly upholding this rule and also because his confusion regarding Sondra didn't allow him to think clearly and wisely he gets caught as a murderer, even though he hasn't murdered.

The lawyers finding a scapegoat like Clyde who out of cowardice and confusion could not remember clearly the incidents which led to drowning, concoct their own stories, to their own advantage. The whole scene moves in a predetermined style leaving Clyde no chance of even reminiscencing whether he was a murderer or no, Clyde doubts that the very fact that he had plotted murder, was by itself a sin. During the trial scene Clyde is so passive and readily exploited by the scheming lawyers that one wonders whether he could have really fallen in love with not one, but two women at a time.

Clyde meekly assimilates all advices very readily during the trial that it seems inconsistent with the plotting and scheming which is attributed to him. Swayed by emotions to escape a nerve racking situation of escaping from poverty and Roberta to Sondra and wealth, he plans haphazardly, totally unaware of the consequences. But the clever, crafty and powerful lawyers infer details from situations in which no inference is intended. The trial from start to finish had been unfair. Prejudice and bias had governed its every step. Such bullying and browbeating and innuendo as Mason had indulged in before the jury would never pass as fair or adequate in any court.[13]

During Jephson's examination of Clyde he not only calls him a moral and mental coward but he also very convincingly and ironically adds:- "Clyde -not that I am condemning you for anything that you cannot help. (After all, you didn't make yourself, did you?)[14] Here the speech in brackets is highly revealing and the irony is that if Clyde is not responsible for what he is, then it means that society is responsible for having made him what he is, at the given point of time.

Clyde's mother is middle aged, homely, determined and religious lady who wishes to prove her son's innocence at all costs. Unfortunately for Asa Griffithe, Clyde's father, the whole thing appears mysterious and beyond his comprehension and he "was unable to grasp even a tithe of the meaning of this."[15]

So Clyde is caught between two extremes -one where there are people like Mason and Jephson who are reading to commit meanings to situations where- in no meaning was intended, on the other hand is Rev. Asa Griffiths so innocent, meek and humble who cannot understand the case at all. Having been brought up by such innocent parents, it is no wonder that Clyde is not able to think clearly and gets confused very soon.

Clyde is ashamed of his past that he had conveniently forgotten it. When asked to narrate his past he is literally groping in the dark because he had allowed himself to be entrapped in a new mechanical way of living engendered by society, that the past is silly, meaningless and to a point shameful. He could never forgive his parents for having been wandering preachers because people of high society did not do it.

Also it is quite surprising how ladies of a wealthy background manage to keep their identity secret. Miss Sondra is referred to as "Ms.X" throughout the trial scene, whereas every letter and every action of Roberta had been exposed very clearly. This exposure clearly attracts the public because of the sensational reading it afforded. The lawyer Mr. Mason appeals to the sexual and moral prejudices of the audience :

> Roberta's letters. . . being described in detail, -even excerpts of some of them the more poetic and gloomy being furnished the press for use, for who was there to protect her. And on their publication a wave of hatred for Clyde as well as a wave of pity for her - the poor lonely country girl who had no one but him and he cruel, faithless, - a murderer even.[16]

The letters which Mason reads at the close speech which he delivered, are enough to arouse the audience emotionally. They are ready to believe that the judges would be justified in executing a death sentence because he had not taken care of Roberta at a crucial moment when she needed him most. She needed his assurance that everything would be fine, but Clyde simply deserted her. Unfortunately Clyde is not to be blamed fully for this behaviour. He is of the opinion " that she has "fallen" and is therefore sullied," while his idealization of "Sondra requires that he divorce his love for her from sexual desire."[17]

As a bell-hop,Clyde is quite fascinated by the hotel, its

rooms, its telegraph office, its taxicab office, and the fashionably dressed men, women and girls who were all a source of attraction to him. He also admired the wraps, furs and dresses which the ladies wore and was keen enough to observe : "This then, most certainly was what it meant to be rich, to be a person of consequence in the world -to have money. It meant that you did what you pleased."[18]

Unfortunately Clyde stands to be misguided by this last statement where he felt that he could also do what he pleased. It is here that his calculation is wrong, for, he should have also remembered that he would have to reap the consequences. Anyhow his experience at Green Davidson arouses the spirit of adventure and he gets interested to go out and venture into the world, to enjoy more of it.

When Clyde received tips at the hotel, he also knew that he could hide this money and use it for his own entertainment and pleasure. Even though he is quite sensitive and full of emotion, he seems to have no sense of direction or rather he is guided by his friends in the wrong direction. "Wasn't he making more money than anyone else in the family? And couldn't he begin to do as he pleased?"[19] In doing as he pleased Clyde finds himself strongly attracted to a girl who was "bright, vain, engaging and so truly pretty." To him her eyes, seemed to have, a kind of "dancing fire in them."[20]

Hortense is a worldly wise girl who knows that she could "capitalise her looks and charm" (P. 102) This love affair is in direct conflict with his duty towards his sister Esta who has been seduced and deserted while she was pregnant. Esta is in need of money for her delivery, while Hortense allures him and tries to secure a fur coat from him. While Clyde is angry with the seducer of Esta for having left her in a pathetic condition, as for himself he is inclined to behave in the same irresponsible manner with Hortense. He wishes to have sexual relationship without any sense of commitment to Hortense. At the same time his sister is shunned because he fears that by paying attention to her he would lose his chance of procuring and consummating with Hortense.

This incident is quite important in the novel. The crude, insensitive manner by which he also deserts Roberta at her moment of utmost need is significant and we are no longer surprised when he wishes to desert Roberta for winning Sondra. There is lack of compassion in his character and it is highly ironical that Clyde who was himself angry with the seducer of Esta should himself be the cause of anger of irrepressible mobs. The crowd could have lynched him while he was being questioned by Jephson at the witness' stand.

According to Donald Pfizer, Clyde was always caught between "duty" and "desire"[21]. There is his duty towards Esta which he avoids in order to win over Hortense. In the automobile accident, when a child is hurt, he is torn between his conscience urging him to rescue the child, and the calls of desire urging him to flee from the scene so that he could live a happier life. At such moments Clyde appears so naive and attractive amidst a vile world pulling him in different directions. While he is bitterly sore at what had been done and while he desperately wishes to connect the situation there arises hope and desire to distract and draw him away from the right path.

When there are two options Clyde becomes nervous, distracted and transfixed and he is unable to act. This is exactly what happened when Roberta fell down when the boat capsized and was overturned. There were two options to save her and live a life of poverty or to let her drown and hope for a brighter, prosperous life , like the one he had witnessed and dreamt of obtaining while at Green Davidson. Having stood indecisively helpless for a moment Clyde chose the path of hope and desire.

In a capitalist society rules are made with the benefit of the factory owner or hotel owner in mind. Breaking rules could destroy the life of a worker. Clyde had enjoyed full laxity and sexual freedom while at Green Davidson because hotels do not restrict such activities. Actually hotels stand to gain more customers by such amoral means.

Clyde entered his uncle's factory from such a background. In the factory, rules were rigid and such intermingling of workers with supervisors was not allowed. They maintained a hierarchy and people were allowed to move only within the social circle to which they belonged. If Green Davidson corrupted the young lad by allowing too much sexual freedom, in the factory lack of such freedom was quite detrimental to Clyde's interest. However viewed, society was at odds with Clyde's interest. Clyde was actually interested by the fact that the girls were pretty. In chapter 14 Dreiser clearly depicts the social taboos attached to working girls.

> For there was a local taboo in regard to factory girls aspiring towards or allowing themselves to become interested in their official superiors. Religious , moral and reserved girls didn't do it ... She soon discovered the line of demarcation and stratification between the rich and the poor in Lycurgus was as sharp as though cut by a knife or divided by a high wall. [22]

If Clyde was seized with the ambition of rising in society, Roberta was "seized with the virus of ambition and unrest that afflicted him" (P. 250) While being attracted by Roberta, Clyde could only perceive her outward charm, grace, simplicity and openness and not her strong and powerful character. Not only was she charming and graceful , she was also a determined girl with conservative opinions of life and marriage unlike Clyde. It is this strength of Roberta's character -her sincerity and total dedication to Clyde which makes a powerful character. Her character is clearly exhibited in her letters also and she is able to create waves of sympathy and admiration even after death.

It is quite ironic and unfortunate that Roberta who was suffused with delight on realising that Clyde loved her and wished to have a fulfilling relationship with her, should be left in a watery grave a few months later. The beginning of their relationship is quite poetically expressed by Dreiser. For Roberta the knowledge of Clyde's interest in her made her feel as if "All the dry marshes and cracked and parched banks of her soul - the dry rivulets and streams and lakes of misery that seem to dot her being - were as instantly flooded with its rich up welling force of life and love."[23]

Little was she to know that all this would end as if it were as ethereal as a dream. Clyde was also aware that his relationship with Roberta was a sin but again his sexual frustration urged him to be drawn by chemic impulses which were strong enough to destroy him .According to Donald Pfizer,

> *The American Tragedy* is thus a novel of the twenties not so much in its external trappings as in the relationship of some of Dreiser's basic themes to the major fiction of revolt of the period. Like Hemingway, Lewis and Fitzerald, Dreiser depicts the falseness and destructiveness of such American illusions as the faith in moral abstractions, the implicit virtue of small-town or rural life, and the association of one's noblest dreams with a wealthy girl. [24]

The pathos of the novel *An American Tragedy* lies in the fact that this story which appears to be a mere story of crime and punishment at the surface level is actually the story of Clyde's development of his psyche. According to Freudian philosophy all impressions right from childhood, work as a whole into the making of a man. It is unfortunate that no one can really penetrate into any man's heart to know in detail all the events of his past life that have grown and multiplied to give him his present shape .

Clyde himself feels harrassed because unfortunately no one believes him. He has no one, whom, in any of his troubled and tortured actions before that time saw anything but the darkest guilt apparently. And yet he has a feeling in his heart that he is not as guilty as they all seemed to think. After all they had not been tortured as he had been by Roberta with her determination that he marry her and thus ruin his whole life.

As for the people who were judging him, he felt that they had not been harassed, tortured, mocked by the ill fate of his early life and training, forced to sing and pray on the streets as he had been forced to in such a degrading way, when his whole heart and soul cried for better things. How at all could they judge him?

It was unfortunate that even the Reverend Mcmillan who enters his life to relieve him of his suffering by making him confess the truth, is unable to understand him and actually fails to ease him. No one grasps the intensity of his feeling and his "mental, physical and spiritual suffering."[25]

Reverend Mcmillan fails to save Clyde by explaining that he had not actually committed murder even though he had contemplated on it a great deal. Mcmillan could have saved Clyde from the electric chair had he understood his longing to live and enjoy worldly pleasures. Ironically, the priest is too spiritual to allow him to live.

As for his close relatives and employers the Griffiths, they also isolate themselves on receiving the news that he had got himself enmeshed in a messy affair. They are also careful to avoid branding him as insane because that would ruin their future prospects. As for Clyde there are streaks of nervousness and it is quite a plausible explanation that his love for Sondra had prevented him from saving Roberta. Here ironically we find that his parents' preachings were to blame. They who had taught him, ."God's will be done,"[26] had never taught him to Judge and act on his own, to fend for himself. He had failed to rescue Roberta and in the process rescue himself from disgrace and self destruction. The way society Judges him is quite peculiar. Each one evaluates him from his own point of view. According to Mizruchi,

> The lawyers see Clyde legalistically, judging his responsibility for his actions; the public see him moralistically, insisting on the necessary repression of human instincts and passion in society; the press sees him sensationally, as a figure to incite and feed a bored public's desire for intimacy with lives seemingly more romantic than their own.[27]

So Clyde attracts the attention of all sorts of people intent on judging him according to their own views on life. Ultimately Clyde is discarded as being fit for the death house.Clyde faces a variety of people right from hardened outright criminals who were "crude, sinister or remote" (P.770) to less cruel, harmless criminals. They could relax and play cards or checkers sitting in their own cells by calling out each particular move. Some loudly read novels of adventure, cracked jokes and life seems to be normal until the arrival of the hour of death. So whenever anyone of the prisoners was moved out of his cell to the electric chair, the rest of them "cried, prayed, lost their minds." {P.771) Clyde was also to face such a fate; but he need not have had to face, had the world viewed him sympathetically in all totality of his experiences, rather than in pre- determined moral, social and ethical codes.

Amidst all the dreadful atmosphere of the death house Clyde's reminiscence on whether he was to blame for all this and if so where lay his weakness is quite heartrending. In quite a simplistic manner Clyde observes :

> Was it not also true that if he had led a better life - had paid more attention to what his mother had said and taught - not gone into that house of prostitution in Kansas city -or pursued Hortense Briggs in the evil way that he had -or after her, Roberta-had been content to work and save, and no doubt most men were - would he not be better off than he now was? But then again, there was the fact or truth of those very strong impulses and desires within himself that were so very, very hard to overcome.[28]

At this moment Clyde's basic necessity is understanding and acceptance. Even though Rev. Mc. Millan and his mother are able to afford it to him to some extent, even they are unable to peer deeply into his soul and understand his needs. Clyde is therefore a lonely sufferer, facing his doom on his own. Even here in the prison, there seems to be a ray of hope that after death there would be peace and calm in the world to come. Unfortunately nobody could rescue him from the chair which stood firmly in front of him.

Dreiser never budged or refrained from ridiculing the pretensions of religion. Even though both his mother and Reverend Mc.Millan remind him to turn to religion for solace, Clyde does not really get any peace of mind. Both the prison and institutionalized religion are cruel in that they bind one's psychic thoughts without offering any respite. The outpour of questions that arise out of Clyde' mind,

> I know I am not wholly white. Oh, no,I know I plotted evil. Yes,yes,I know that. I confess.But must I really die now? Is there no help?Will you not help me,Lord?... Will you get the governor to change my sentence before the final moment to imprisonment?....I will drive out all sinful thoughts.[29]

Despite all such out pouring, Clyde is not thoroughly convinced that he has gained strength from such soul searching. This is revealed in the following statement. "Mama, you must believe that I die resigned and content. It won't be hard. God has heard my prayers. He has given me strength and peace. " But to himself adding, "Had he?" [30]

This passage clearly shows the hypocrisy of religion. It is not religion which could help him, but at the same time had Rev. McMillan proclaimed his innocence to the Governor, then it would have been a sincere and larger step towards his release and enabled him to enjoy a longer life on earth. This gaping chasm between a person's basic qualities and a careful and sympathetic acceptance of it, is what the world desperately requires. At the moment of death Clyde's eyes were "Fixed nervously and, as he (Rev. Mc. Millan) thought, appealingly and dazedly upon him and the group surrounding him."[31] Rev. Mc. Millan was himself not sure whether he had done right, "Should he have said to him -that perhaps- perhaps - there had been those other influences playing upon him?..." [32]

There is another such incident in *Hey ,Rub-A-Dub-Dub* in which Dreiser has narrated an incident to show how difficult it is to state which is right and which is wrong.

> A girl falls in love with a boy to whom the father takes an instant dislike. The father is not better than the lover, just different ...when the father opposes them they wed secretly. Result, rage. A weak temperament on the part of the father causes him to drink. On sight, in liquor he kills the youth. The law says he must be hung unless justified. A lie on the part of the girl defaming the lover -husband will save the father. On which side now do right, truth, justice, mercy stand ? [33]

Therefore we are skeptical about the administration of so - called justice, for it is quite difficult to decide in such situation as to who or what is right and with whom God is. These passages reveal the crux of the novel *An American Tragedy* that each one had unfairly evaluated a young boy full of vitality , vigour and the compelling urges of youth.

Not only Rev. McMillan, but Clyde's mother also realises her mistake and she is more careful in dealing with their grandson (Esta's illegitimate child) Russell. They feel that they should be more liberal to him and are actually ready to give him a dime for an ice cream cone . At least if not in life, at least after death, Clyde has made everyone understand that children need a balanced life with both love and leniency along with moral preachings. They have a dominating energy and life spirit in them and cannot be harnessed but need to be guided and diverted in the right direction. Suppression would only increase desire and this would result in satiating it by clandestine affair and secretive behaviour.

Dreiser believed that hard and fast rules should not govern people's behaviour, and also that as all men are different one's needs, beliefs or apprehensions need not be the same as another's. But the most unfortunate thing is that the religionists believe that we are all of one mould and keep advicing men to live and follow a uniform code of moral.

> The religionist, the moralist, the editorial writers preach a faith and an obvious line of duty which they label

> grandiosely "right" or "true", "just" or "merciful". My observation and experience lead me to believe that there is scarcely a so called "sane", right, merciful, true, just, solution of anything.[34]

All solutions are relative according to needs and demands of a particular sect of society, of a particular period what is acceptable to one sect of people also need not necessarily be acceptable to another sect. Listing a number of items both man made like jails, detectives, penitentiaries, court of law "to natural phenomenon like fires, deaths and painful births", Dreiser observes that : "All these things are good in the hands of good people, evil in the hands of evil,and nature seems not to care which group uses them. A hospital will aid a scoundrel as readily as a good man and vice versa."[35]

Not only the hospital, but also courts of law. If only Clyde had the money and influential parents like his lawyer Belknap he would not have had to face the electric chair. Instead the story would, have been entirely different, Clyde would have been a free man administering justice to others, may be! Another newspaper item quoted by Dreiser reads thus :

> A priest, having a girl and confessed to it, no way was found to electrocute him because of his cloth. Men whose services and aid he condemned insisted that he must be proved insane and not be electrocuted, though he did not agree with them[36]

Having quoted such items from newspapers Dreiser questions the readers as to where justice is, in such situations? If a priest who is supposed a follow a serious moral and religious code could behave licentiously and still be saved, why not the sensitive, weak, misguided youth, Clyde be accepted by the norms of society?It is noticeable that the operating systems themselves were more at fault than the individual. So Clyde's case is one of succumbing to multifarious pressures of society which act in a variety of ways to ruin him.

In Theodore Dreiser's collection of poems, *Moods* there is a poem entitled "Epitaph". It is actually an epitaph for a girl who used to play the violin for the sick in the hospital, but unfortunately she herself died of pneumonia, unattended and all alone. It is at this instance that Dreiser questions the very existence of God himself.

> Tell me one thing:
> Is this universe ruled
> By a Being who knows pity ?
> (I think not)[37]

Dreiser thus does not believe in a God who is just and sympathizes with the miserable and weak. In another poem entitled "Chief Strong Bow Speaks" Dreiser very confidently proclaims :

> For the Gods are good
> Yet only
> When it is there whim or mood[38]

So if at all something good happens to someone it is just that he has been lucky at that particular instance. Clyde, as we see him right from the beginning is neither a powerful character like Cowperwood nor of an outright artistic temperament like Eugene Witla. So he cannot claim to be exquisitely God gifted. He is just an ordinary, sensitive boy with nothing extra ordinary about him. With all these limitations the novel is so grasping because of Dreiser's simple minded devotion to the central theme of Roberta and her fortunes or rather misfortunes in her relationship with Clyde.

So the novel is unified and as the murder is dealt with in a very detailed manner, it has all the thrill of a present day best seller. To top it all, the novel is a success, because it underlines the defect, or rather questions the American social order as such, and presents it as being defective and improper. In such an order the lives of a section of people is predetermined as compared to that of the elite, who can manipulate situations.

The solution to all the problems faced in the novel is given by Dreiser himself in "A Counsel to Perfection" in *Hey Rub-A-Dub-Dub*. Here Dreiser has elaborately explained how man is helpless in front of chance or fate:

> Man is a waif or accident in nature . . . In so far as one may judge by chemistry and physics man appears to be in the grip of a blind force or process which cannot help itself and from which man can derive no power to help himself say by accident or per adventure. . . The important thing for him to do,...would be to avoid henceforth all destroying notions of this character and to think of himself rather as a waif, an unloved orphan in space, who must nevertheless and by his own effort make his own pathetic way in the world.[39]

Once man understands that he is responsible for his own fate ,he gains the capacity to think and act appropriately without blaming others for his failure. Also having acted on his own decision he should have the courage to face the consequences.

> I ... would prefer to be a seeking Prometheus chained to a rock and my liver gnawed daily by the eagle of an irritated and jealous higher power than a crawling worm whimpering slavé praying for some endless Nirvana, or a minute part of an endless legion of cherubim harping on glory of something which had plainly sought neither my peace nor my significance but only my painful, unimportant and even worthless service .[40]

Having found that the social system and the American dream were responsible for the suffering of the oppressed Americans, Dreiser suggested communism as a panacea for the ills in America. "They have a condition based on the idea of abundance for all and they are trying to achieve their aim, despite the enormous natural obstacles and unnatural ones placed in their path by monopoly -made nations. They are... trying the idea that the man is worthwhile." [41]

If such a system was adopted in America where everything was available in plenty then the catastrophic situation as of Clyde in *An American Tragedy* could not have arisen. Of course while advocating Communism, Dreiser was against suppression of personal freedom by Communists. Dreiser had always been the champion of the underdog of society. It is with this view that he advocates Communism so that the workers as well as the landlord could share profits equally and not that one should get the lion's share leaving nothing for the worker. Dreiser firmly believed that "the pivot of the system would and should be that all must work in order to eat." [42] Here Dreiser is fully convinced of the futility of his earlier theory, "Survival of the Fittest."

Unemployment which was a result of the "Depression" was one of the giant problems which stifled the normal, decent behaviour of youth and therefore it became necessary that even while they were very young, they had to take up jobs as bell hops in hotels as we see in Clyde. Lack of proper food and clothing only made the young boys look pathetically at those who were eating good food or wearing lovely, decent clothes.

Lack of such basic amenities would only lead to psychological problems like an inferiority complex which in turn is hidden under the mask of harshness and impertinence .Dreiser was thus thoroughly disillusioned with the capitalist system which aided a few to rise at the cost of the masses. Therefore Dreiser observes in *Tragic America:*

> My facts and experience I interpret as meaning not only that this is the decadent stage of capitalism, but also that any and all reform is now, in the large, vain... What must come now is something that will synthesize all forms of human effort, but not with the view of making the individual too powerful and certainly not with the view of making him exorbitantly and ridiculously comfortable and showy and intractable, and at the expense of millions who make his pride and his utter intractability possible. The rich are

> too rich; the poor are too poor. And the hour has come when some form of equitable sharing in the means of living -shall not only have to be considered but wisely and truly enforced.[43]

Only when such disparities are dissolved can any reforms be brought about in the condition of the exploited masses. Dreiser's was a sincere and heart felt plea that even Swanberg has observed : "His abstract tenderness for humanity was sincere and sometimes proven."[44]

Another reform which Dreiser has suggested is in the sphere of education. As children were wrongly or partially educated with either an overdose of religion as in the case of Clyde then such fates as his would follow suit. Dreiser has suggested that education should be freed from religion and " should be arranged and paid for by the Government." [45] Children should also be inculcated with a knowledge of their "rights" and they should have to toil for their own bread. Dreiser also insists all people must be made to understand that " Neither the necessities nor the more interesting and pleasurable phases of their lives can be had without the conditions of all the individuals of the world working to supply them."[46]

Only if such proper tutoring is inculcated by children will they understand that money can be got only by intelligence and hard labour and not by philandering with rich women. Once such notions are clear in their innocent minds then the chances of children going astray would get minimized and such tragedies like the one Clyde was exposed to would be reduced.

NOTES AND REFERENCES

[1]Dreiser, *Tragic America*,1.

[2]Dreiser's letter to Harrison Smith. April 25, 1931.

[3]Dreiser, *An American Tragedy*(New York: New American Library, 1981),14.

[4]Dreiser, *An American Tragedy* ,48.

[5]Dreiser, *An American Tragedy* ,308.

[6]Dreiser, *An American Tragedy* ,309.

[7]Gerber, *Theodore Dreiser Revisited*,86.

[8]Dreiser, *An American Tragedy* ,272.

[9]Dreiser, *An American Tragedy* ,400.

[10]Dreiser, "Four cases of Clyde Griffiths" New York Times Clipping, n.d. (U.P.)

[11]Dreiser, "Four cases of Clyde Griffiths",806.

[12]Dreiser, "Four cases of Clyde Griffiths",396.

[13]Dreiser, "Four cases of Clyde Griffiths",738.

[14]Dreiser, "Four cases of Clyde Griffiths",675.

[15]Dreiser, "Four cases of Clyde Griffiths",743.

[16]Dreiser, "Four cases of Clyde Griffiths",5.

[17]Pfizer, *The Novels of Theodore Dreiser*,236-237.

[18]Dreiser, "Four cases of Clyde Griffiths",47.

[19]Dreiser, "Four cases of Clyde Griffiths",57.

[20]Dreiser, "Four cases of Clyde Griffiths",100.

[21]Pfizer, *The Novels of Theodore Dreiser*,243.

[22]Pfizer, *The Novels of Theodore Dreiser*,249-250.

[23]Dreiser, *An American Tragedy* ,299.

[24]Pfizer, *The Novels of Theodore Dreiser*,218.

[25]Dreiser, *An American Tragedy* ,798.

[26]Dreiser, *An American Tragedy* ,25.

[27]Susan, L. Mizruchi, *The Power of Historical Knowledge* (New Jersey: Princeton University Press, 1988),283-284.

[28]Dreiser, *An American Tragedy* ,784-785.

[29]Dreiser, *An American Tragedy* ,807.

[30]Dreiser, *An American Tragedy*,809

[31]Dreiser, *An American Tragedy* ,811

[32]Dreiser, An American Tragedy , 811

[33]Dreiser, *Hey Rub-A-Dub-Dub* ,9

[34]Dreiser, *Hey Rub-A-Dub-Dub,*10

[35]Dreiser, *Hey Rub-A-Dub-Dub,*11

[36] Dreiser, *Hey Rub-A-Dub-Dub,*13

[37]Dreiser,"Epitaph" A Poem From *Moods,*173

[38]Dreiser, *Moods,* 185

[39]Dreiser, "A Counsel to Perfection" An Essay in *Hey Rub-A- Dub-Dub* ,123

[40]Dreiser, "A Counsel to Perfection", 125

[41]Dreiser, *America is Worth Saving* (New York: Modern Age Books, 1941) 285

[42]Dreiser, *Tragic America*, 423

[43]Dreiser, *Tragic America* ,84

[44]W.A.Swanberg, *Dreiser* (New York: Scribner's,1965), 416.

[45]Dreiser,*Tragic America*,422.

[46]Dreiser,*Tragic America*,355.

CHAPTER VI

Emergence of his theory of existence

Theodore Dreiser's theory of existence can be said to have emerged in four different stages. The development is very gradual and systematic and shows Dreiser's experiences in life which in turn enabled him to propound his philosophy.

In the first stage, while experimenting with *Sister Carrie* and *Jennie Gerhardt,* Dreiser was not very happy with the out come of events of his life on earth. Young and inexperienced as he himself was, he had a feeling that life on earth was purposeless and useless. He seemed to be

> Attacking the conventional ethical codes which to him seemed to hold men to standards of conduct that had no rational basis in fact, while they condemned others without regard to what Dreiser thought might be the real merits of their situation.[1]

The characters in *Jennie Gerhardt* and *Sister Carrie*, hope to ascend in society and get rid of their poverty, and in the process they promulgate Dreiser's theory of existence. It becomes clear from the example of Sister Carrie and Jennie Gerhardt that while the two of them achieve fame and success, characters like Hurstwood or Senator Brander happen to lose their wealth, position, pride and finally their life too.

Despite all these realistic observations of life, Dreiser was always of the view that even though nature does not always seem good to us, it is not bad. As Lundquit[2] has also mentioned, Dreiser thought of nature in relationship to pervading goodness; but he is not willing to give a conception of evil the upper hand either. To him Nature is wise, avoiding median conditions or strict balances between opposite forces, because this would be nothingness.

Dreiser had always had full faith in Nature and trusted that Nature could bring about a balance in all earthly happenings even though his main theme in *Sister Carrie* is the "purposelessness of life" , he is not quite sure what life held in store for man. The women in both the novels are struggling for existence.

In the second stage of his development Dreiser experimented with "superman" .He seems to have felt that if man's life on earth was a struggle, then the "superman" would definitely make a mark for himself on earth. According to the Darwinian theory of "survival of the fittest",the fittest man is the one who is seen in the *The Financier*, *The Titan* , *The Stoic* and *The "Genius*". He is the man with some internal force prodding him to achieve more and more, but not for long.

Nature definitely controls all affairs and so the towering Goliath also has to grasp the fact that "Giants are but pygmies" in the face of the earth, and so the great financial wizard also faces a lonely death like all other human beings. *The "Genius"*, is also another superman like Cowperwood but instead of being a financier, he is an artist with innumerable paramours . " He is set loose in the turbulence of modern life and permitted to exercise his superior cunning and resourcefulness untrammeled by moral restraints or inhibiting consideration for others."[3] Even with him the equation inevitable occurs and if he has a rise, he also has a fall. Dreiser actually seems to be reminiscensing on the exact condition of man in society, and the individual in the cosmos.

In the third stage of his development, Dreiser seems to have realised that all social evils can be done away with, only if all men unite together to fight against it. *An American Tragedy* is a superb example of what society can do to an individual who is naive, inexperienced and misguided. Society directs him to the electric chair without bothering to verify the various circumstances which were instrumental in bringing about his ruin. Social disparity, dubious morals and conventional religious beliefs were all detrimental to the uplift of society. So in the third stage, Dreiser's main concern is with thoughts of adopting socialism as a panacea for all ills.

> In *The Financier* , *The Titan* and *The "Genius"*, Dreiser saw life through the eyes of a superman, to whom it appeared as a welter of forces among which he must try somehow to work out his individual salvation. The damage to society in the career of a Cowperwood may be discovered in the books; but the purpose of those books is not to dwell upon the social evil of his career. Similarly Eugene Witla's career is seen as an individual's struggle.... In Clyde Griffiths' progress on the contrary, social implications abound. His (Dreiser's) *American Tragedy* is a tragedy brought about by the society in which we live. That society is the immediate cause, for Clyde's actions... Clyde's tragedy is a tragedy that depends upon the American social system.[4]

Finding capitalism and the desire to accumulate more and more wealth as the root cause of all suffering, Dreiser preferred socialism which, he felt could augur well for the poorer section of society and help in uplifting the downtrodden.

In Dreiser's report in *Dreiser looks at Russia* he has not exactly approved of the Communist principles as such because there were no equal right for everyone either socially, politically or economically. Also there is the lurking idea behind everyone's mind that he is being watched as everyone is looked upon as being a spy. There's no freedom even in the sphere of art as one is made to feel that any work of architecture should be functional, also any performance in the theatre should be educational. No Russian feels that he should work for himself alone; but his notion of any project is a collective effort. There are chain hotels, chain stores and chain newspapers in America also but in Russia collectivism is so deeply ingrained into the system of the people that they fail to feel enthusiastically regarding work. So Dreiser feels that communism is also not the solution for America.

The fourth and final phase of Dreiser's life is when Dreiser realises the harmony and oneness of the universe and the fact that true happiness can only arise out of universal love. In Dreiser's acceptance of the universe as such, there is, "A sensation of cosmic understanding, of an overarching sense of unity with the world in its apparent evil as well as in its obvious good."[5]

From the initial sense of incompatibility of mind and reality, Dreiser has ultimately graduated to a "transcendental mind with its passionate sense of oneness."[6] As Dreiser himself has stated in one of his lectures, "What I believe" in 1929,

> I still rise to testify to the aesthetic perfection of this thing. . . which we call Life . . It can and does achieve an aesthetic whole -beauty no less -and via the same elements that are in lice and bedbugs as well as in the most distant suns or sidereal systems - in fire and flowers, in Shelley and Christ.[7]

In an essay entitled "The toil of the Labourer" in *Hey ,Rub-A-Dub-Dub* Dreiser was bemoaning the condition of a labourer who had to work like a machine in order to make both ends meet. Yet despite all their hard labour nobody recognized their importance in society and it seemed that they were deemed to live a life of wretched poverty and isolation. At the same moment a realisation dawned upon Dreiser that may be this disparity was quite essential to society, for variety adds charm to life.

> And yet sometimes when I looked out upon the world as it glimmered before my windows when I saw it so chanced, the waters of the river flowing by, the splendid boats riding at anchor or steaming peacefully past, and the wonder of the hills and hollows, all set suggestively before the eyes -it came to me that, perhaps, in spite of the seeming injustice involved in this situation, and the very inequalities, I was bemoaning were the things which I was admiring in Nature.[8]

Referring to the theory of evolution, Dreiser has observed that man has actually evolved into a complex being from simple things. In his essay "Equation Inevitable" in *Hey, Rub-A-Dub-Dub,* Dreiser has observed, "...that life in every form has tended to evolve from the simple to the complex, and only through a vast complexity or organization has it managed to attain this spectacle of things which we call life or beauty- division of itself as it were."[9]

In this process the less strong have got wiped out and only the more vital or complex species have remained in this world and they express themselves in various ways. So in case men wish to live in harmony with his neighbours, "There is the contrary fact that these schemes are constantly being interfered with by contrary forces, decays, mistaken notions, dreams which produce in harmony."[10]

So everything is balanced in nature. Religion or belief in God is only a balm which provides soothing relief when mishaps occur."If you have nothing better to do even a religion may be worthwhile. At worst it can only narrow your vision, and if that is a comfort -well, it is a comfort, but you do not thus escape the essential facts of life."[11]

Having no faith in the preaching of religionists or moralists because their theories do not hold good as far as the universe as the whole is concerned; for instance Dreiser's argument is that if man is to be classified as beggar, robber or lecher then what about all the disease causing microbes and bacteria which work havoc on man, the image of God, without the least consciousness of God, or equation or anything else.

> I am thinking of the germs of cholera, smallpox. . . which while destroying vegetation, and wealth most necessary to man at one point at the same time may and do nourish birds inimical or helpful to him and cause all things to develop methods of defending themselves and so their growth.[12]

All these are a matter of equation according to Dreiser "force with matter, element with element" (P. 158) and so on. As all religions or morals are a matter of convenience or rather selfishness, as man desires happiness only for himself and not to co -exist with all the variety of creations present on earth, Dreiser's observation is that, " If you observe him carefully you will find that in the main he desires so-called"justice" for himself only, a fair balance for himself, liberty for himself, or that which is related to him via pleasure or profit, and so on, ad infinitum."[13]

> Men like Rockefeller or Napoleon do not follow any ethical codes and "nature seems to have no objection to them or their results."[14] Even though man has written a lot of books with spiritual instructions in them, not all are followed nor can he forcefully enforce all his theories, he cannot accommodate all of them because, Nature, his sheer, rank human nature, which sinks deep below into mechanistic, chemical and physical laws and substances will not let him. . .The fact is that the power of certain individuals to do is only limited by the power of certain other individuals to resist. . . The self - integrating force of one individual is limited by the self integrating force of all other individuals; which is, if it is anything, Newton's law working out in human affairs .[15]

It has also been observed that if some men "fight and die" (P.165) for moralistic or idealistic beliefs there are others who die for materialistic ends. So the equation continues. Man himself slays animals, fishes and a number of other creatures so that he could be comfortable and spiritually at rest. In such a situation, where is the "Universal harmony" , or justice" or "mercy"? And from where do the rights of the universe come in, which each of us hope to "rob to our own advantage?"[16] and that too by enslaving all other creations of nature which are under our control.

In this beautiful world of ours all animal forms care for their young, are distressed by their loss and are also capable of organizing themselves and observing group laws. It is Dreiser's observation that,

> ...These lower forms cannot possibly know of religious or moral precepts in any revealed or instructed sense, via a Messiah or Redeemer. Instincts or tropisms as developed to and verified by opposition or, aids.. .appear to have been their sole guides.[17]

Life as it is, is "neither too good nor too bad" wherein order and disorder co-exist and as far as human beings are concerned, "Strife is the only key to knowledge or sensation and life that we have."[18] So man should go on striving for more knowledge and the universe will reveal more and more wonderful creations as it were.

> Under this same controlling equation, a man may be a Colossus and bestride the world without upsetting the equation ultimately. Like Alexander, he may sigh for more worlds to conquer, or, like Hannibal, take refuge in despair and death. Or, better yet, like some forceful and yet humble labourer at some small task, he may seek to hide himself away in some simple peaceful realm, free of the storms which rock these greater worlds,and still be secure in one of those minor equilibriums which in the shadow of source of the greater ones are always holding somewhere in part.[19]

Whatever man does in this earth there is this equilibrium ever present in all his activities. So whether it is a lover's love for his beloved, or a child for his mother or a citizen towards his neighbour, or even hunger and its happiness, insatiation are all exemplifications of the harmonious equations in life. "Life builds and wills far beyond the ken of man or his companion animals, and all that he can know is the chemic thrill of life, its joys, the necessity of equation and so called fair play, or rythm and balance."[20]

So life can best be understood only if looked upon it in its totality and not as individual aspects. What had actually happened in the seventeenth and eighteenth century was that some descendants of Anabaptists, Quakers and Moravians had brought forth strains of pietism among uneducated classes in Europe .

> Pietism involved a rejection of human tradition and authority, a reliance on personal experience, and the enthusiasm of those who felt they were shaking off dry, old forms and were penetrating to the inner mystery of things.[21]

So far so good.Unfortunately, instead of moving towards atheism and secular reform they managed to "Lift God to an inscrutable height" and man was left helpless in a "determined universe." [22] As a reaction to such a thoroughly depressing and fatalistic belief a group of individuals who were, "Worried about human pride and selfishness"[23] tried to work out a vision of sanctity or happiness through harmonizing the self with the inevitable flow of events. These men preached a love of being in general, of humanity for its own sake rather than for changing moral virtues. Christianity preaches a love for the unlovely, and according to the pietistic psychology, the poor and the socially immoral were not necessarily the worst sinners. They preached that if ordinary love and virtue were the results of natural law, then true virtue consisted only in the acceptance of the universe as a whole, and that only in such an acceptance can there be universal happiness .

Dreiser also believed in the fact that universal love is the key to all happiness. These ideas have been very clearly revealed in two of his later books -*The Stoic* and *The Bulwark*.Dreiser had already revolted against any religion, right from childhood as he felt that it was all formal rites, no history, geography or algebra. It has so many dogmas which could neither be verified and children, he felt were being corrupted by religion. There is a highly pathetic example of religion being unable to help Clyde from having to face the electric chair in *An American tragedy*. Clyde's mother was desperately hoping against hope that god would aid her in her hour of need.

Clyde's mother's last hopes dwelt on the Governor's judgment and when approached, the governor also refused to act from a religious point of view or with sentimentality as it was a legal case. Religion therefore fails even in this instance. Clyde himself was pathetically expecting to gain some sustenance from religion, while in prison. "Clyde was now doing what every other human in related circumstances invariably does - seeking, and yet in the most indirect way, the presence or existence at least of some superhuman or supernatural personality or power that could and would aid him in some way. . . ."[24]

Unfortunately all this was in vain as no god could guide him or show him the way to Life and Happiness once again. Even in his personal life, Dreiser had had certain bitter experiences with religion that he was put off by Catholicism. When Dreiser's mother expired the priest from the Holy Church insisted that, "the church would not bury her in the consecrated ground because she had not been a faithful Catholic lately."[25]

The poor lady was all the time busy settling down and fending for the children that she hardly had any time to go to church but that was stated as a reason for her not being given a place in the churchyard, after death! Such pettiness which he experienced from religionists made him lose all faith in religion or convention also for that matter.

There is a change in Dreiser's mode of thinking in his novel *The Stoic* .In this novel Dreiser is drawn towards Hinduism. This is evident in his turning Berenice of *The Stoic* into a Yogi. Berenice understood the meaning of pure spirit, Brahma and finally the realisation of Divine Love. Berenice's stay for four years in India is dealt with quite seriously by Dreiser. Berenice's behaviour denotes Dreiser's own "leap from pure matter to pure spirit."[26] The Guru's instructions to Berenice that, "No human being can give up action altogether, but he who gives up the fruit of action is said to be non attached,"[27] shows Dreiser's own understanding of the philosophy of the *Bhagavad Gita.*

The secret of regulated breathing aiding one in getting rid of desire and the instruction to only do good for goodness' sake are quite awe- inspiring not only to Berenice but to Dreiser as well. As for the Lord, Berenice is told that he can be experienced through the heart and not through the intellect.

The Guru's instructions enabled Berenice to admire beauty in the Hill of Ramtek where there were temples and the whole surrounding resonated with the chanting of mantras. The idyllic setting made her heart pulsate with admiration. She studied Pranayana -the control of the vital forces of the body; Pratiphara - or making the mind introspective; Dharana, or concentration and dhyana or meditation. She also understood the fact as explicated by the Upanishads that Brahman is Existence, knowledge, and Bliss and that Brahman is not wise or happy, but "absolute knowledge, absolute Joy." [28]

So Dreiser here understood that man on earth should strive for more and more knowledge in a very detached manner. Also Dreiser got an idea of the evolution of different species on this universe in a very cyclic manner.

> There is nothing new. The same series of manifestations are presenting them selves alternately, like a wheel coming up and down. All motion in this universe is in the form of successively rising and falling. Systems after systems are coming out of the finer forms, evolving themselves, taking the grosser forms, again melting down, as it were.[29]

Dreiser also understood that souls are immortal; only that the soul leaves the body and enters another body. So there is neither birth nor death but a continuity of existence. As we are never born and we never die, each atom is a living thing, leading its own independent life. These atoms combine into groups for an end, and the groups manifest a group intelligence so long as it remains a group, these groups again combining in turn and forming bodies of a more complex nature, which serve as vehicles for higher forms of consciousness. When death comes to the physical body, the cells separate and scatter and that which we call decay sets in. The force which held the cells together is withdrawn, and they become free to go their own way and to form new combinations. Therefore death is but an aspect of life, and the destruction of one material form is but a prelude to the building up of another.

When atoms get attracted towards one another, there occurs what can be termed as Divine Love or God or Hari, as he is known in Sanskrit , is omnipresent and he initiates attraction of one object for another. As he is present everywhere, even the so called lower animals are a reflection of the Divine Love or Brahman or Reality. "We think we worship beauty, but we are really worshipping the face of Brahman shining through. The reality behind the scenes."[30] There is also the idea of "making" and "unmaking" .The idea of making suggests Brahma the creator and the idea of unmaking suggests Shiva, the destroyer. Actually Cowperwood worships beauty in God,when he admires Berenice, the embodiment of beauty.

In order to realize God, Berenice is told to free her mind of all delusions, then she would see God in all manifestations on earth. When this love of God grows to a great size it becomes supreme devotion. In this state,

> Forms vanish, rituals flyaway, books are superseded, images, temples, churches, religions and sects, countries and nationalities, all these limitations and bondage fall off by their own nature from him who knows this love of God. Nothing remains to bind him or fetter his freedom.[31]

In this ultimate state of liberation, the soul would also become free or liberated. There is sheer unalloyed happiness or sheer Bliss. Berenice had understood that Cowperwood's Love for her which was a "Constant search for beauty in every form, and especially in the form of women, was nothing more than a search for the Divine design behind all forms - the face of Brahman shining through." [32]

Berenice also put to practice all that she had learnt in India. On returning to America, she felt miserable to see starving children suffering from malnutrition, neglect and disease and remembered the Guru's advice that "by helping a poor man, you are able to help yourself. For is not the universe yourself?" [33]

She immediately began to complete Cowperwood's unfulfilled task of building a hospital for undernourished and ailing children, thereby visualizing God in man. Instead of thinking about her own social status, she started thinking about a vocation which was socially worthwhile. So only in the process of moving outside the self to the universe can one realise the meaning and spiritual import of life. As Dreiser has himself once observed in his *A Hoosier Holiday*,

> I once believed, that nature was blind, stumbling force or combination of forces which knew not what or whither. . . Of later years. I have inclined to think just the reverse, i.e. that nature is merely dark to us because of her tremendous subtlety and our very limited powers of comprehension.[34]

Theodore Dreiser was also impressed by the totality of the universe like Whitman or Emerson. They wished to explore the universe in all its wholeness and move from individual to society. In the preface to a story entitled "Giff" an account of a spiritualist known to him, Dreiser has stated thus:

> In the fact of all inductive science and the strange yet narrow walls of all naturalistic philosophies... I hold that behind the seemingly foolish predictions which "came true" moves something which is ...solidly real ... an all pervasive intention or plan.[35]

Dreiser had always tried to seek out this plan of nature and always felt that whether it was religion or conventions or morals they should all relate to the universe as a whole and not deal with it in bits and parts. The Quest for the mystery or secret of life was always a preoccupation in Dreiser's mind. In this connection he had collected a lot of material. In one such note in his "The Mechanism called Man" Dreiser has observed,

> The secrets of energies that make the plants and animals grow ... Energy-electrical energy - passing along the nerve cells to the veins and arteries provide the command or pressure which holds them normally controlled, giving the same rate and quantity of flow, throughout the entire body. Is this mental or a mechanical procedure? If it is mechanical what is the nature of the force that controls electricity and causes it to serve, as it does. [36]

Here Dreiser has a feeling that all such mechanical forces which we see are controlled by a higher force "The nature of God,or the creative force that appears to operate directly through matter - energy as well as the laws and spatial conditions environing the same is, in fact the one reality- universal creative reality."[37]

Having recognized this fact that there is a "universal creative reality" Dreiser then began to see a scheme and radiant beauty in all God's creations be it the star or a tiny little worm. There was beauty in all evolutions of life. So in an essay entitled "My Creator" Dreiser's observations are as follows:

> I am moved not only to awe but to reverence for the creator of the same whom his presence in all things from worm to star to thought - Imeditate constantly. Awe I have . And at long last, profound reverence for so amazing and aesthetic and wondrous a process.[38]

Dreiser also had made -references to astrology, palmistry or religious prophecies and superstitious beliefs. An astrologer in *The "Genius"*, predicts Eugene's ups and downs in life and a palmist predicts serious troubles followed by success. Not only these, the society of Dreiser's time also believed in superstitions. Dreiser's mother herself believed in them. Having seen three phosphorescent lights bobbing towards her across a meadow, Sarah Dreiser, his mother believed that her three sons would die and all died in three years.

Dreiser himself had some belief in certain signs and omens. Dreiser called them the "system of occurrence"[39]. According to Miyoko Takeda, Dreiser saw a certain kind of person just before the operations he had at different times. He saw hunchbacks on some occasions. Each time they heralded his meeting with a certain person. A Jew always appeared at the critical moment for Dreiser, on trains or aboard ship in New York, in Chicago and in the south.

There are very many instances of telepathy also in Dreiser. During a trip to Indiana, Dreiser had a car accident and the very recollection of the same brought forth another accident once again. Also there is a note in George Fox's journal in which Dreiser has pointed out how George Fox who was in prison in Lancaster, could feel the pain of the Quakers being executed in America even though he did not know about their execution.

Dreiser also had a firm belief that human suffering is because of ignorance and improper utilization of available resources. In his book *A Hoosier Holiday* Dreiser has described his trips to Indiana, and finding the soil quite fertile there, he wishes that those who are living in unfertile soil should be transported there. Instead of wasting one's time in just thinking, Dreiser wishes that man should live his life fully and intelligently. Dreiser was always upset by the fact that life is filled with contraries but all the same, it requires adjustment and acceptance to face life with equilibrium and live a fully useful life.

> In society, where a man is constantly scheming out methods of procedures and how his ideas and feelings and appetites can be brought to a harmonious workable state... the need of striking a balance or achieving an equilibrium between plainly restless and conflicting elements.[40]

In order to bring about such an equilibrium human beings need to have a fertile imagination and the capacity to dream: "Dream on. Believe. Perhaps it is unwise, foolish, childlike, but dream anyhow, "for" of dreams and the memory of them is life compounded." [41] Even in this book *A Hoosier Holiday*, Dreiser has expressed his faith in the existence of a larger power which, "Appears beneficent . . . something so large and strange and above our understanding"[42] and that man can improve his lot by a change of outlook and that the masses should thrive and progress, only then would the individuals stop exploiting them.

Somehow Dreiser was staunchly of the opinion that each human being should work and reap the fruits of his own labour and not enjoy the fruits of his ancestor's labour, doing nothing.In addition, Dreiser was of the firm opinion that there should be strict discipline and the society should not be like an undisciplined jungle.

> ...It is by Nature and evolution intended as such, for certainly the thousands -of -years -old growth of organized society augurs desire on the part of Nature to avoid the extreme and bloody individualism of the jungle.[43]

Theodore Dreiser who was quite fascinated by the Quaker ideal has written *The Bulwark* with the Brotherhood of Quakers in mind. The Quakers are of the staunch view that they should help each other in their hour of need. Dreiser wished to obtain a "classless brother - loving society" [44] by religion.

Unfortunately the younger Barnes' find it too very difficult to reconcile themselves to the world of religion in contrast to the materialistic world at large. Rufus Barnes and Hannah are contented and complacent as long as they are in their little town of Maine; but then shift to Philadelphia and the luxurious mansion of Hannah's sister Phoebe, and bring forth visions of luxury and pleasure in the minds of the younger Barnes. Having once tasted luxury it is naturally difficult for the youngsters to strictly follow Quaker ideals. Some Quakers were even abandoning Quaker brotherhood in order to live a luxurious, materialistic life. But Solon Barnes the elder son of Rufus Barnes remained aloof. To him all that mattered was a clean life with straight forward dealings. He saw, everything in terms of divine order...a "series of law governed details, each one of which had the import of being directly connected with divine will... To him the religion of George and John Woolman was the solution of all earthly ills."[45]

It is no wonder that once Solon finds that the other bankers are bent on making large undue profits which are against his Quaker ideals, he quits the job. Personally he himself had brought some property for speculative purposes and had also made some profit in its resale. But he is shattered at his own behavior which he felt is unjustly ambitious and religious.Quakerism or no Quakerism Dreiser's concern had always been with the underdog of society. In a poem entitled "What to do?" Dreiser has observed,

> And one, the lover of his fellow man says Take, from each according to his ability; Give, to each according to his need.
>
> And so from the heart comes the answer of him who does and serves
> That by degrees,
> A new and better world
> May be made.[46]

Solon seems to embody these ideas of Dreiser's and having read the *Book of Discipline* he is sternly of the view that, "When any become possessed of ample means , they should remember that they are only stewards who must render an account for the right use of things committed to their care." [47]

In sheer contrast to Cowperwood who hoards money, Solon's heart is with the poor and his opinion is that the banks should work for the uplift of the poor and not ruin their lives by forcing them to pay exorbitant rates of interest. Throughout the novel there is the conflict in Solon's mind between his own faith in simplicity and society's materialistic attractions.

Solon Barnes' faith is too intricate and impossible a deal

for his offspring. For his son Stewart "girls were uppermost in his thoughts at this time"[48] and for him the embodiment of life were "showy, half dressed chorus girls", "gilded youths" and "men about town". Revolting against his father's stern, strictly moralistic ideals and unable to understand the meaning of "Inner light" Stewart yearns for immediate self gratification and elopes with a girl. Unluckily for him a friend of his, mixes opium in the girl's drink and she dies. Stewart's involvement is noted and he is arrested but unable to tolerate the shame, he commits suicide.

Solon's daughter Etta fares no better. Frustrated with life, as a result of too much discipline, she runs away to New York where she leads an immoral life. Hers is an unhappy love affair with a painter and she feels thoroughly dejected and depressed.

Stewart's death and Etta's depression thoroughly deprive Solon of any happiness at home. Solon understands that his children have been victimised by modern society to which Quakers of the last quarter of the nineteenth century had fallen prey to. The plight of Quakers is clearly depicted in the following lines by Rhoda Wallin in *The Bulwark* .

> I haven't a thing against the Quakers. I love them dearly. If I could live as they do, and keep my place in society, I'd do it. But it can't be done, Stewart, I can't do it, no one can. How can you give up music and dancing and theatres and looks and motion pictures and fit into the world of today? It can't be done![49]

This summarizes the attitude of the younger generation towards the strict discipline imposed on them by their parents. Rhoda also comforts Solon on the death of Stewart stating that the world has changed since they were children. There were not so many "diversions and temptations" (P. 297) then and so the children were not to be blamed and that Stewart was trapped by circumstances and had not committed evil intentionally.

Stewart's death is a shattering experience for Solon whose

mind is unable to accept the fact that his son had succumbed to the pleasures of modern society. It is then that Solon contemplates and propounds Dreiser's philosophy that, "We were motes, atoms, electrons...we were Part of a whole ,everything was a part of a whole, chemically, electrically and also philosophically."[50]

Robert Elias has called the novel, *The Bulwark* as "a kind of tribute to the creative force,"[51] because Solon was desperately searching for a meaning of this universe. At such moments Solon used to walk up and down in the garden; as a child, Solon used to feel that God was closest to Nature. Etta who had returned home to overcome her own afflictions, was also beginning to realise that tranquillity of mind and happiness could arise only from serving others; and she begins by remaining close to her father in his moments of crisis.Observing the various aspects of Nature right from fish, birds, butterflies and grass, Solon experiences a kind of religious awe and wonder. One day Solon noticed a green coloured fly, which was as beautiful as an emerald perched on a bud and devouring it .This made Solon wonder, "Which was intended to live -the fly, the bud, or both?"[52]

Solon got the answer to his question very soon. One day, during a walk he closely observed Nature and after bending down and examining a blade of grass here, a climbing wire there, a minute flower, lovely and yet inexplicable as his green fly, he turned in a kind of religious awe and wonder. He learnt there must be a Creative Divinity, and so a purpose, behind all of this variety and beauty and tragedy of life "Tragedy had descended upon him, and still he had faith and would have".[53]

This indomitable faith in the scheme of all creations in Nature is what makes Solon realise that one should love all God's creations. Surprisingly Solon encountered a puff adder and his experience with it made him feel that he could communicate with animals also. The adder had raised its hood and was ready to strike. But Solon decided to speak to it and did so, telling it that he knew that it was harmless and that it could go its way without harm or interruption from him,at which, it reduced its swelling neck to normal, lowered its head and proceeded to depart. Then, wishing to know how long it really was, he took two or three paces forward in its direction, and again it spread its neck, and lifted its head, cobra fashion. Then he talked to it again, saying that he would not follow it or harm it in any way. At this point he retraced his steps and paused again to observe its departure. Then it turned and went back towards him, crawling so close so as to cross the toe of his shoe.

This incident clearly expresses Dreiser's philosophy that all God's creations are part of a whole and it only needs a bit of love to understand one another and communicate with each other. Solon explained to his daughter that if we reach out with love, then all God's creations would reach out in the same manner .

> I mean that good intent is of itself a universal language, and if our intention is good, all creatures in their particular way understood, and so it was that this puff adder understood me just as I understood it... My intent being not only good but loving, it understood me and had no fear, but came back to me, crossing the toe of my shoe. I thank God for this revelation of His universal presence and His good intent toward all things -all of His created world. For otherwise how would it understand me, and I it, if we were not both a part of Himself? [54]

Etta, while serving her father by reading works of John Woolman to him had understood that what really mattered was love. She had also understood that through her service to him she could see what it might mean to serve others, not only for reasons of family bonds or personal desires, but to answer human need and help all humanity.

Etta clearly grasped the fact that by loving God, love began spreading further and further, "To the poor,the weak, the slaves, the miners." [55] So there was no end to love, it was universal extending from man, to flowers, to insects and even snakes. In this love and unity with all nature, as she now sensed, there was nothing fitful or changing or disappointing - nothing that glowed one minute and was gone the next. "This love was as constant as nature itself, everywhere the same, in sunshine or in darkness, the filtered splendor of the dawn, the seeded beauty of the night. It was an intimate relation to the very heart of being.[56]So love is a constant and ever fixed status and therefore can easily be grasped by one and all. All that is needed is an open mind to admire different aspects of Nature and extend our love to it.

Dreiser's observation in "A Counsel to Perfection" is that on an average man has around seventy years life span and even though it appears as if, "He is an accidentally evoluted mechanism or minute tool in the hands of something more significant than himself that he is as nothing"[57] ,he should not succumb to such feelings of hopelessness but should rise and strive to make his life worthwhile for he should understand, "that his life here is something which is to be lived here and now to the utmost, in the best form for all." [58]

In order to live a happy life here and now, he should reject all vain theories that man is born to suffer and so on and he should try and live life in such a manner so that he enjoys himself and allows others also to enjoy themselves, as joy for himself depends upon his joy in others and they in him. The same thought is more elaborately elucidated in Solon's speech in *The Bulwark* , when he is fascinated by the adder and when he is convinced that it was his own good intent which brought forth good intent in the adder,

> . . .Many things which I thought I understood, I did not understand at all. God has taught me humility -and, in His loving charity , awakened me to many things that I had not seen before. One is the need of love toward all created things.[59]

It is this humility and love which made Dreiser perceive the existence of God in all existing creatures in this universe. So Dreiser had conceived of God and understood him in his own way. "It was God conceived, discovered and accepted"[60] through his own imagination, effort and experience. As an incorrigible individualist, he therefore convinced that choice and decision of religion ought to be left to the individual, he created for himself his own God. It may be "the universe" or "the vital force" or "Thoreau" or "Christ" or, even, "the Mind" .Whatever it may be, it transcends everything; emancipates everything, and settles itself above human beings: it is "the Inner Light".

Dreiser also felt that all human beings who exist on this earth Living life to the lees was what he was interested in, amidst all its.variety and disparity. On the one hand, Dreiser's father who was a moralist and preacher was demanding that all creatures of the world return to Christ and the Catholic Church, but on the other hand there were such miserable scenes in nature which made Dreiser question whether all this religion was worthwhile in such an atmosphere.

> Why did Nature, when left to itself, devise such astounding slums and human muck heaps? Harlots in doorways or behind windows or under lamp posts in these areas ...and this in the heart of this budding and prosperous West, a land flowing with milk and honey! what had brought that about so soon in a new, rich, healthy, forceful land - God? devil? Or both working together toward a common end? [63]

Dreiser's awareness that while one part of the world is deprived, suffering, ruined the other half cannot gain happiness, peace or spiritual elevation. It is this humanism in Dreiser that has found expression once and again in all his works. Dreiser was sensitive and quite perturbed to witness misery anywhere and in any form.

> I was filled with intense sympathy for the woes of others, life in all its helpless degradation and poverty, the unsatisfied dreams of people, their sweaty labours,the things they were compelled to endure - nameless impositions, curses, brutalities the things they would never have, their hungers, thirsts, half formed dreams of pleasure,

> their gibbering insanities and beaten resignations at the end. I have sobbed dry sobs looking into what I deemed to be broken faces and the eyes of human failures.[64]

Such a sensitive soul could definitely not have resigned himself to gain comfort and solace from religion. Commenting on his father's predicament, Dreiser is particularly careful to note that after wasting all his energy and life preaching religion his father was left alone, isolated, to fend for himself in his old age. If religion could not guarantee family comforts and happiness during old age, then what was its worth? To Dreiser religion was something deeper, more sincere and more substantial. Unlike his father's religion which did not even secure him filial devotion in his old age, Dreiser was interested in the Quaker principle of interdependence which quoted by Solon from Woolman's journal is as follows:

> A principle placed in the human mind, which in different places and ages hath had different names; it is however pure and proceeds from God's.- It is deep and inward, confined to no forms of religion not excluded from any, when the heart stands in perfect sincerity. In whomsoever this takes root and grows, they become brethren.[65]

This universal brotherhood or oneness is what Dreiser wished to follow. When all creatures identify themselves one with the other then they can co -exist or else all life forms on earth shall consume or destroy one another and get wiped out of existence. So according to Sidney Richman in his article Theodore Dreiser's "*The Bulwark:* A Final Resolution" ;

> It was therefore not the form or forms of religion that gave truth, but the truth behind all such forms ..If the rituals of worship differed, true religion wiped out all distinctions. Whether it be the passion of the Communist, the Quaker, or the writer, the effort to improve man's condition was simply an extension of that principle of God awakened in the human soul.[66]

Dreiser had written a poem entitled, " what to do" in which he has elucidated how in a period of war all men unite to get together and strive for the betterment of the world.

> "The small -town editor, "the worker's
> Friend", "the educator" and the "minister"
> All work to improve the condition of the world.
> And so from the heart comes the answer
> Of him who does and serves
> That by degrees
> A new and better world
> May be made.[67]

Dreiser's main objective as a writer was to create an awareness in men that our main goal in this world should be to strive for its betterment and live with a feeling of oneness. In a poem entitled, .'Epitaph" Dreiser has clearly elucidated this point:

> The Unborn
> As well as the born
> The dead
> As well as the living
> All ancient newness
> As well as new decay
> And age, youth
> As well as youth, age
> Yet newness fearing decay
> Only the dying are resigned to it
> The dead go back to it
> Yet all suspended
> In its blind
> And dubious
> Oneness.[68]

At this point it would not be improper to quote Swami Vivekananda to show how all Indian philosophers had been preaching the same idea of oneness over and over again.

> Here is the world, and it is full of misery. Go out into it as Buddha did,and struggle to lessen it or die in the attempt. Forget yourselves; this is the first lesson to be learnt, whether you are a theist or an atheist, whether you are an agnostic or a Vedantist, a Christian or a Mohammedan. The one lesson obvious to all is the destruction of the little self and the building up of the Real Self.[69]

Speaking of the "unity" in "variety" which is the plan of the universe, Swami Vivekananda observes: "As a man you are separate from the animal but as living beings, man, woman, animal and plant are all one and as existence you are one with the whole universe. That universal existence is God, the ultimate Unit is the universe. In Him we are all one."[70]

In Dreiser there is a gradual shift from his view point in *Sister Carrie* where Carrie is left all alone in a rocking chair dreaming of things that may never come true, then there is the Superman, Cowperwood "who even after accumulating loads and loads of wealth, dies alone but his actual philosophy of existence is explicit in Berenice's behaviour, when she realises that it is not by living for oneself but in living for others that one gains happiness. This idea is further illustrated in his *The Bulwark* where Dreiser depicts the universal oneness between all living creatures. The transformation was brought forth by a life full of experiences, from a coal picker, to a newspaper boy, to a writer of novels. World Politics also added to his experience and made him the great novelist that he had become.

It was unfortunate that there were such hindrances to human progress such as religionists, materialists and moralists that Dreiser is forced to question: " When will we lay aside our swaddling - clothes, enforced on us by ignorant, impossible puritans and their uneducated followers, and stand up free - thinking men and women?" [71]

Dreiser's career as a journalist gave him an opportunity to come into close contact with men and women and to know them quite clearly. Influenced by Spencer, Dreiser knew quite clearly that life was full of conflicting forces. So whether it was Eugene Witla, Cowperwood or Solon Barnes they were all balanced by counter forces operating against them. The reality behind all life is that all men wish to work for advancement but instead of the advancement being materialistic as in Cowperwood if it were to become advancement of society in general, then there would be universal peace and happiness .

Dreiser's poem also depicts his *Moods* and gradual advancement of moods to realisation of the truth of life.

Despairs;
Each and all,
As in a song,
As in a dirge
As in a great sob of misery
Or sigh of indifference
Or contest;
You,
I
All things
To what future?
In what forever?[72]

These moods of questioning the mystery of the world continued for quite a long time until at last he got the answer to it. In "The Aspirant" Dreiser questions once again,

Meditate
Upon the stories
I would like to make
The places
I would like to go
The things
I would like to see,
And brood
Upon the insoluble question

Of Why? [73]

After undergoing suffering and working hard to realise the mystery of life he got the answer to his questioning in *Sutra.* So whatever realisation Dreiser had received was from his reading of Indian or rather Vedic Philosophy and *The Bhagawad Gita.*

Hail then - King of Blessedness.
The light of mankind.
For you are the many, in one -
The One in many - the absolute.
The very songs of the morning stars are yours
And the shouts of men [74]

At this point I am reminded of a sloka from the *Purusha Sookt* in the Vedas where the lord is described thus:

Sahasra Seersha purushaha !
Sahasrakshaha sahasrapath [75]

(The lord is described as having a thousand heads, eyes and feet, meaning that he is omnipresent in all creations of the earth.)

In the eleventh sloka of the fifteenth chapter of the *Bhagawad Gita* there is a verse which describes the lord as being established in the self, but reveals himself only to sages, and the unintelligent and unrefined even though striving do not behold him.

Yatantoyoginascainam pasyantyatmanyavasthitam!
Yatanto pyakrt atmano nainam pasyantyacetasah![76]

(The lord is thus prevalent everywhere and it only needs a prepared mind and eye to perceive him.)

All these ideas are revealed to Berenice also in *The Stoic* when the *Yogi* preaches to her thus:"You are not educated when merely you are well -schooled. You are truly educated only when you are enlightened by inner truth", [77] the same idea has been explicated by Dreiser in his poem entitled "Related" wherein the inner truth or universality of experience is revealed.

> This exquisite moment
> Of pulsating relationship
> Here
> Now
> Rock
> Flower
> Tree
> Beast
> Rain
> Calm
> Sound
> Heat
> Cold
> This companionship
> Here and now
> With wind
> And sun
> And Sea
> Gases
> Forces
> This integrality
> In variety [78]

Dreiser had always perceived an "integrality in variety", the Cosmic oneness, and right from childhood he had been a simple, frank, honest, outspoken and humble being and could therefore guide and elevate all his readers to the ultimate realisation of the purpose of existence of earth. Vera Dreiser had pointed out in her essay "Some Reflections on Dreiser" that even as a school boy he had written the following poem :

> I would not give the bells that ring
> For all the world of bartering
> Nor yet the whispering of the leaves
> For all the gold that greed conceives

To me the grass that grows in Spring
Is sweeter than fame's offering
And ah! the smile of kindly worth
Than all the wealth of all the earth [79]

The philosopher in him had begun blooming even as a child. No wonder it had culminated in his old age with his reading of Eastern Philosophy and the *Bhagavad Gita.* Dreiser's idea of evolution and involution as expressed in his *The Stoic* also have an echo or parallel in Swami Vivekananda's lecture entitled "The Cosmos" which was delivered in New York, 19th January 1896.The following is an excerpt from Swami Vivekananda's speech:

> The mountain comes from the sand, and goes back to the sand; the river comes out of vapour; and goes back to vapour; plant life comes from the seed, and goes back to the seed; human life comes out of human germs, and goes back to human germs. ..Out of what has the tree been produced? Out of the seed... The whole of the tree was there in the seed . Every evolution is preceded by an involution. The seed is the father of the tree, but another tree was itself the father of the seed. The seed is the fine form out of which the big tree comes, and another big tree was the form which is involved in that seed. The whole of this universe was present in the cosmic fine universe.[80]

The same idea is revealed in the Upanishads also where it is stated:

> Anudwena mahatvena dwitha dishtati keshavaha

(God is manifest as the smallest of small forms and as the biggest of big forms.) Dreiser has also expressed the same idea in *The Stoic* when Berenice gets spiritual guidance from an Indian Guru.

> The seed is becoming the plant; a grain of sand never becomes the plant...What was the seed? It is the same as the tree. All the possibilities of a future tree are in the

> seed; all the possibilities of a future man are in the baby; all the possibilities of any life are in the germ... we find that every evolution presupposes an involution... From the lowest protoplasm to the most perfect human being, there is only one life. The design is inherent in the seed before the form is evolved.[81]

Thus Nature would only produce that which is inherent in itself and nothing else. So by insisting on Puritanic ethics or Darwin's theory men cannot thrive, but they can thrive only if there is an atmosphere of security, humanism, aesthetic insight,universal love, and a devotion to serve society compassionately, allowing mankind to bloom and prosper.

NOTES AND REFERENCES

[1]Charles Child Walcutt, *Modern American Fiction* (Ed. by A.Walton Litz, O.U.P., 1963),50.

[2]James Lundquit,*Theodore Dreiser*,112.

[3]Walcutt,*Modern American Fiction*,60-61.

[4]Walcutt,*Modern American Fiction*,63.

[5]Kazin and Shapiro.*The Stature of Theodore Dreiser*, 144.

[6]Kazin and Shapiro, *The Stature of Theodore Dreiser,* 137.

[7]Kazin and Shapiro, *The Stature of Theodore Dreiser,* 236.

[8] Dreiser, *Hey Rub-A-Dub-Dub*,97.

[9]Dreiser, *Hey Rub-A-Dub-Dub*, From the Essay in "Equation Inevitable",166.

[10]Dreiser, *Hey Rub-A-Dub-Dub*,158.

[11]Dreiser, *Hey Rub-A-Dub-Dub*,177.

[12]Dreiser, *Hey Rub-A-Dub-Dub*,From the Essay "Equation Inevitable",159.

[13]Dreiser, *Hey Rub-A-Dub-Dub*,174.

[14]Dreiser, *Hey Rub-A-Dub-Dub*,162.

[15]Dreiser, *Hey Rub-A-Dub-Dub*,163.

[16]Dreiser, *Hey Rub-A-Dub-Dub,* 168.

[17]Dreiser, *Hey Rub-A-Dub-Dub*,172.

[18]Dreiser, *Hey Rub-A-Dub-Dub*,178.

[19]Dreiser, *Hey Rub-A-Dub-Dub*,177.

[20]Dreiser, *Hey Rub-A-Dub-Dub*,From The Essay in Equation Inevitable,180.

[21]Kazin and Shapiro,*The Stature of Theodore Dreiser* 226.

[22]Kazin and Shapiro,226.

[23]Kazin and Shapiro,226.

[24]Dreiser, *An American Tragedy,*785.

[25]Dreiser, *Dawn,*519.

[26]Walcutt, *Modern American Fiction*,65.

[27]Dreiser, *The Stoic*,291.

[28]Dreiser, *The Stoic*,293.

[29]Dreiser, *The Stoic*,295.

[30]Dreiser, *The Stoic*,297.

[31]Dreiser, *The Stoic*,298.

[32]Dreiser, *The Stoic*,307.

[33]Dreiser, *The Stoic*,305.

[34]Matthiessen, *Theodore Dreiser (*Dell Publishing Co., 1966), 239.

[35]Pfizer, *Critical Essays of Theodore Dreiser,* 324.

[36]Pfizer, *Critical Essays of Theodore Dreiser,* 326.

[37]Pfizer, *Critical Essays of Theodore Dreiser*, 327.

[38]Pfizer, *Critical Essays of Theodore Dreiser,*327.

[39]Miyoko Takeda, *The Quest for Reality of·Life*, (New York: Peter Lang Publishing Inc, 1991),82.

[40]Dreiser, *Hey Rub-A-Dub-Dub*,From The Essay "Equation Inevitable",157.

[41]Dreiser, *A. Hoosier Holiday(*New York: John Lane & Co., 1916),512.

[42]Dreiser, *A Hoosier Holiday*,368.

[43]Dreiser, *Harlan Miner's Speak* (New York: Harcourt, Brace & Co., 1932),16.

[44]Dreiser, *Dreiser Looks at Russia*,49.

[45]Dreiser, *The Bulwark* (New York: Doubleday, 1946) 90.

[46]Dreiser, "What to do" Free World (IX March 1945),10.

[47]Dreiser, *The Bulwark*,38.

[48]Dreiser, *The Bulwark*,195.

[49]Tjader, *Dreiser. A New Dimension*,65.

[50]Tjader, *Dreiser. A New Dimension*,65.

[51]Elias, *Theodore Dreiser, Apostle of Nature*, (New York, 1949),304.

[52]Dreiser, *The Bulwark*,37.

[53]Dreiser , *The Bulwark* ,317.

[54]Dreiser , *The Bulwark* ,319.

[55]Dreiser , *The Bulwark* ,331.

[56]Dreiser , *The Bulwark* ,331.

[57]Dreiser, *Hey Rub-A-Dub-Dub*,116.

[58]Dreiser, *Hey Rub-A-Dub-Dub*,120.

[59]Dreiser, *The Bulwark*,319.

[60] Atsuko Takashima, *Essays and Studies in British and American Litt* (Vol. I No. I: 1959),99.

[61]Dreiser, '*The Bulwark*,337.

[62]Dreiser, *Dawn*,8.

[63]Dreiser, *Dawn*,60.

[64]Dreiser, *Dawn*,92.

[65]Dreiser, *The Bulwark*,328.

[66]Pfizer,*Critical Essays on Theodore Dreiser*,334.

[67]Pfizer, *Critical Essays on Theodore Dreiser*,334.

[68]Dreiser, *Moods*,183.

[69]Swami Vivekananda, *The Complete Works of Swami Vivekananda* (Advaita Ashrama, 1976),353.

[70]Swami Vivekananda,381.

[71]Dreiser , *Hey Rub-A-Dub-Dub*,276.

[72]Dreiser, *Moods. Cadenced and Declaimed* (New York: Boni and Liveright, 1928),70- 71.

[73]Dreiser, *The Aspirant* (New York: Random House, 1929).

[74]Dreiser, *Moods*(New York. 1935),316.

[75]*Purushasooktham* (Madras: Ramakrishna Math),3.

[76]*The BhagavadGita* (Gorakhpur : The Gita Press) 303.

[77]Dreiser, *The Stoic*,291.

[78]Dreiser, *Moods*(New York: Boni and Liveright, 1928),70-71.

[79]Dr. L. Jegannatha Raja, *Theodore Dreiser: The man and his message*,96.

[80]Swami Vivekananda, *The complete works of Swami Vivekananda*,205-208.

[81]Dreiser, *The Stoic*,296.

CHAPTER VII

CONCLUSION

John Mc Aleer has observed about Theodore Dreiser that "throughout his life, Dreiser experienced steady intellectual growth."[1] I would like to add that it was not only an intellectual growth, but it was an emotional and spiritual growth — emotional because he was emotionally attached to his country and so has boldly depicted the weaknesses in American society; spiritual, because there is a very gradual but definite spiritual growth, from the self to the universal as revealed by his novels. Sister Carrie's or Jennie Gerhardt's search for a job depicts the universal struggle for existence but Solon's acceptance of a snake as indeed a creation of God and having a soul like humans is a universal acceptance of all living creation as kin to one another. One is reminded of Emerson's "Rhodora" wherein the poet is enamoured by a flower "Rhodora" and expresses thus: "The self-same power that brought me there brought you."[2]

Like Emerson or Thoreau who were quite deeply influenced by Hindu scriptures , *The Bhagvad Gita* and the Upanishads, Dreiser was also influenced by Buddhist and Hindu scriptures. While in India Berenice of the *The Stoic* is instructed on matters like Raja Yoga and Hatha Yoga. The idea in *The Stoic* that Brahman is absolute joy and that the entire universe is pervaded by the Lord and that all creatures exist in him have been obtained from the *Gita* and the *Upanishads.* Verses 28,29 and 30 of chapter VI of *The Bhagavad Gita* contain such theories.

> Yunjannevam sadatmanam yogi vigata kalmasah I
> Sukhena brahmasamsparsam atyantam sukhamashuteII[3]
> [The sinless yogi thus, uniting his self constantly with God, easily enjoys the infinite bliss of oneness with Brahman (the Absolute). (28)] The idea of the self present in all and all beings in the self is in the following verse of the *Gita.*

Sarvabhutasth aatmanam, sarvabhutani catmani I
Iksate yoga yuktatma sarvatra samadarssanahII[4]

[The Yogi whose mind is harmonized by Yoga, looks on all with an equal eye, sees the self present, in all beings and all beings existing in the self.(29)] Verse 30 of the same chapter also contain a similar idea.

Yom am pasyati sarvatra sarvam ca mayi pasyati I
Tasya ham na pranasya misa came na pranasyatiII [5]

[He who sees Me(the universal Self) present in all beings, and sees all beings existing in Me, I am never out of sight of him, nor is he ever out of sight of Me(30)]

So whether it is persons, animals, birds, things or incidents, God is present in each of them and all of them are present in God. It is no wonder that in *The Bulwark* , Solon is able to perceive a oneness with a puff adder. "Donald Pfizer has made a note of the fact that Theodore Dreiser used to carry a copy of the *Bhagavad Gita* with him." [6] According to Vedic philosophy also the whole world is regarded as one unit or family "*Vasudeiva Kutummbakam.*" Also he (God) can be visualized as the smallest of the small atoms or the biggest of the big objects in the world.

Anoraniyanmahato mahiyantatmasya janato.[7]

Hindu philosophy abounds in such thoughts. It is quite surprising to find that from the materialistic world, Dreiser has evolved to realise the sheer uselessness of money and power and that only sharing gives man supreme Bliss.

This quest or search for a meaning in life, understanding his relationship with other men, his relationship with nature and the Universe was what had preoccupied Dreiser throughout his novels. Whitman's "Song of Myself" also has a similar thought : "What is a man anyhow ? What am I? and what are you? In all people I see myself, none more and not one barley corn less."[8]

So the idea of oneness has been prevalent in Dreiser's age

and he has also used it in his works. Dreiser's quotation of Emile Bronte's poem in *The Stoic* goes on to prove that instead of vacillating and doubting goodness on earth he had come to believe in it.

> Though earth and man are gone
> And suns and universes cease to be ,
> And Thou were let alone,
> Every existence would exist in Thee.[9]

Dreiser has graduated from the feeling that there is grief, sorrow, materialism, to the fact that all experiences on earth transport us to eternity. Dreiser has graduated from the purposelessness of existence on earth to the realization and belief that as souls are eternal, our existence on earth, along with other creations on earth is also eternal.

Unlike Buddhist philosophy which harps on the fact *Sarvam dukham, dukham; sarvam kshanikam, kshanikam*,[10] that everything is sorrow and that everything is momentary, Dreiser has eternalized joy by universalizing our experiences. If there is beauty in the rose then all of us are beautiful because the rose is also a part of us and we are a part of the rose. The very experience of happiness on viewing a rose is enough to make our visages glow with happiness and in turn beauty emanates. Dreiser was also aware of the beauty in variety and the fact that it is Nature which makes and regulates man, and that she makes him any way she pleases- "vile, lovely, strong, weak, simple, complex and so on."[11]

To the sensitive and rational writer, Dreiser, the mystery of the universe was always of great interest. Even though Dreiser was not quite convinced about God's existence in the beginning, later on he got quite convinced of the existence of God in all creatures on earth; but what delighted him most was the beauty and harmony in this universe.

Once on viewing a cluster of wild yellow flowers- near a laboratory, Dreiser was delighted to note how stunningly

> beautiful they were and exclaimed that there must be a divine, creative Intelligence behind all this "Not just a blind force" , but a great "Artist" , who made all these things with such love and care . . . . . After that he began to feel differently about the universe. He saw not only the Intelligence, but the love and care that goes into all created things.[12]

Earlier Dreiser was quite disturbed to see what man had made of man. But later on he was comforted and rather delighted to find that the world in which we live is rather stupendously admirable and attractive. "Dreiser was of the view that all nature is regulated by something (God is one word also Spirit, *Brahma*, divine essence, or Force)."[13] Elsewhere in a poem entitled *Sutra* Dreiser has praised God and identified him as being present not only in nature but also "in the shouts of men."[14]

Identifying God and soul as being one and the same, Dreiser was able to perceive superb and supreme Bliss existing when one lived in harmony with Nature. After having passed pungent and acrid remarks on America and its materialistic society Dreiser was able to come to terms with the universe and view it in the right perspective.

Dreiser's opinion was that the moneyed class were able to sway power and utilize police, judiciary, press and church also in their favour. Police power was for "corporate benefits as opposed to labour interests"[15] and the law also leaned in favour of the moneyed classes. It was then that he observed, that "The rich are too rich; the poor are too poor and that hour has come when some form of equitable sharing in the means of living-shall have to be considered and truly enforced."[16]

This does not mean that Dreiser liked his people to follow a communistic spirit. Dreiser liked Russian law because it did not encourage accumulation of wealth. The people were working for the uplift of all. Dreiser was not totally enraptured by their system also because he felt that they had no privacy whatsoever: "You live too many in one room and are even lunatic enough to identify it with acommunistic spirit. I rise to complain. And I suggest in this connection that more individualism and less communism would be to the great advantage of this mighty country..."[17]

Dreiser was soon disillusioned regarding the belief that individualism was best. This was because individuals who were stronger, tactful and wiser reaped all the benefits and deprived the other weaker ones from gaining anything substantial. Even the church was rather inefficient in encouraging the weaker section to awaken and explore the possibility of survival. So the weaker ones in society, Dreiser feels, are totally subjugated by preachings of the church,politically, socially and otherwise. They count on its power and influence as of use to them. Its "revealed wisdom counsels resignation and orders faith in a totally inscrutable hereafter. " In short, it makes for ignorance and submission in the working class. And this is what a "corporate-minded government" or "financial group" , desires "complete control of everything for few". [18]

Not all men can be scheming, tactful and successful, some would definitely be like Dreiser himself ambitious but easy going and pleasure loving. "Therefore instead of taking to heart the emphasis in our home and elsewhere on the need of energy, study of a practical character,ambition, self-denial and some other things in order that one might properly prepare oneself for the battle of life, I was for mooning about and dreaming of how delightful it would be to be this and that, have this and that - without effort - by luck or birth, as it were."[19] Dreiser was at the same time afraid of having to may be meet with failure enroute. He was quite aware of the actual condition of society around him and the wretchedness of men weighed on him and he would ponder over the suffering and the hunger in New York and its "crowded tenements" , the "sick babies" , and "the people sweating under undue loads" on summer days and he empathised with the women who were "sewing, sewing, way late into the night."[20]Philosophers, intellectuals and artists were rarer compared with tycoons in America. Dreiser has always felt that Americans were weaklings artistically, intellectually and philosophically whereas financially and commercially they were most powerful, almost giants, and men like Rockefeller, Gould, Sage, Vanderbilt the first, H.H.Rogers, Carnegie, Frick have become "freaks in the matter of money getting."[21]

Dreiser was particularly aware of the fact that this craze for wealth did definitely ruin some while it encouraged some to struggle hard and succeed. So one needed to exercise caution while adhering to this search for a successful career. Even of Cowperwood of *The Titan,* Dreiser was of the view that he himself was not responsible for his fate. It was society and social beliefs and necessities that led him to destruction. If the society had not admired such people then such tycoons would never have existed. "Who plans the steps that lead lives on to splendid glories, or twist them into gnarled sacrifices or make of them dark, disdainful contentious tragedies? The soul within? And whence comes it? of God?" [22]

Here Dreiser's opinion is that the society which can make and break laws is responsible for creating Cowperwoods. There is a passage in *Sister Carrie* also which shows how society enables a rich man to rise to the top by very readily getting engaged as workers. Comparing a man's progress to his bodily growth, Dreiser observes that men either grow stronger, healthier, wiser, like the youth who is approaching manhood, or "weaker, older, less incisive mentally" like the man approaching old age. This is quite natural. But businessmen get saved from "dissolution of fortune" by hiring younger brains. So in case such young men do not help the older factory owners then "his fortune would pass as his strength and will. He and his world would be utterly dissolved and scattered into the four heavens." [23]

By sheer manipulation of the needs of society some men are able to rise to become successful individuals. Instead of trying to rise financially if men could develop an artistic vision then society would definitely advance in the real sense of the word. It was his concern for society which made Dreiser request society to resist actively and successfully the illusions of mental and spiritual growth or achievement through the amassing of material wealth or "earthly distinctions, honors or powers". These are the things that are to be actively resisted, by refusing to succumb to their allure, and instead, in their place, "to cultivate moderation, simplicity, self-restraint, and repose."[24]

There is a parallel to this thought in *The Bhagavad Gita* Chapter VI verse 4.

> Yada hi nendriyarthesu na karmasvanusajjate I
> Sarva samikalpsamnYasi yoga rudhastadocyate II [25]

(When a man ceases to have any attachment either for the object of senses or actions and has renounced all thoughts of the world, he is said to have attained yoga.]

Influenced by such spiritual philosophy, Dreiser has observed in *Sister Carrie:*

> It is the higher mental development that does away with such thoughts. It is the higher mental development which induces philosophy and that fortitude which refuses to dwell upon such things refuses to be made to suffer by their consideration . . . It is the unintellectual miser who sweats blood at the loss of a hundred dollars.[26]

This monetary consideration did not allow many potentially great men to flourish as artists. Dreiser has remarked in an interview in 1914 that people never dreamt that greatness could be achieved as a writer, a musician, an artist. Therefore all the"potentially great men poured into business." [27] Such craze only weakened their spirits and made unsuccessful ones commit suicide and become neurotic. So there was no good literature or art worth the name during Dreiser's period.' According to Dorothy Dudley in her "Dreiser and the land of the free," "Big business movements are making it impossible for men to express themselves as individuals because they can not hope to succeed in small enterprises they have lost their initiative and their power to think."

Also she adds that the quest for money had made men nothing but asses. "Modern business had made American citizens into nothing but trudging asses."[28] In such a materialistic world men cannot help but go crazy. Dreiser has tried to save the nation from such a total neurotic collapse by his novels. The social awareness which he has created is nothing short of any Mahatma or wise soul speaking to the masses. It was with an intention of liberating and freeing souls that Dreiser had written his novels. America could only be saved from ruin if men were able to realize that a perfect vision and not perverted values could save America from disaster. If men were to dream of suppressing one another in order to become lord and master, nothing concrete and substantial could be achieved from such a situation. Men like Eugene Witla of *The "Genius"* were of the following opinion: "Not to wince, not to quail, but to stand firm, square to the world and to make people obey. Oh, what splendid a vision of empire was here before him."[29]

If everyone was to dream such a dream then there would be only one selfish class,but if everyone was to think of helping each other sharing gifts as well as sorrow with one another, there would then be happiness which emerges out of universal brotherhood. Instead there was discontent and unhappiness all around. As Dreiser himself has pointed out the main problem with millions of people in America, is the worry as to where food and bed are to come from. And they strive for these until death ends the struggle. "The battle is that of man against man, group against group, trust against trust, but all fighting the individual."[30]

Such a drastic situation cannot be attributed to any development or advancement as such. There can only be depression, deterioration and devastation of the millions. Dreiser is of the firm view that a capitalistic society is not a successful one and he added that: "The fundamental principle-that all of the necessities resulting from the comparatively advanced stage of invention which has been attained should be given to all people equitably for their services or labor - has been, in the main, disregarded."[31]

This disregarding of the basic humanization ideal which

distinguishes human beings from animals is a cause for concern and rectification. Moreover the more and more powerful financiers were able to threaten and force institutions as well as governments to bend to their will. "For business, through politics, certainly dominates in America today."[32] There was "no honest or worthwhile labor leadership in America; politics and legislative bodies aiding and abetting the few at the expense of the many, and so making for loss, confusion, and as we see now, even national as well as financial futility."[33]

The same idea has been repeated in *Hey ,Rub-A-Dub-Dub* in an essay entitled "Life, Art and America" where he grieves over the absurd condition in which politics, religion or trade was in America.

> Politics, as I found in working as a newspaperman, was a low mess; religion,both as to principles and its practitioners, a ghastly fiction based on sound and fury, signifying nothing; trade was a seething war in which the less subtle and the less swift or strong went under, while the more cunning succeeded; the professions were largely gathering places of weaklings, mediocrities or mercenaries, to be brought by, or sold to,the highest bidder.[34]

Dreiser has actually practised what he preached his materialistic and money minded brother — the businessman. He preached that the businessman should in case he had leisure time "question the things he sees - not some things but everything - stand, as it were,in the center of the whirling storm of contradiction which we know as life, and ask of its source and its import."[35]

Dreiser has done exactly what he has preached. Throughout his life he had been questioning the object or the reason why we were born as human beings. To contemplate life at large and understand its purpose , meaning and intention is what Dreiser desired every individual to do.Once when told by a Philosophy Professor Hugh Miller that "Science can and must pursue religious truth in order to advance " [36], Dreiser took the matter seriously and then started defying and questioning a mechanistic view of life. Dreiser observed :

> You can't tell me there's no meaning in those little roots reaching out toward the nourishment that's in the soul. I'vestudied the thing under a microscope and I tell you it's not just a machine. There's something more than we had thought in this process by which these plants grow and add life themselves.[36]

So the most important aspect of Dreiser is his firm belief in personal observation without depending on books or other aids of knowledge. As Dreiser himself has observed in his *A Book About Myself* he was a self-made man and proudly deserves to be called so. "And as I grew, I began to note that personal observation and deduction were far more valuable to me than any book. And so I continue to think to this day, although I am by no means dismissing books as aids to my own observation."[37]

Dreiser's own observation, aided by instinct made him what he was. Telepathy, superstition and instinct are also found in his novels. As he himself declares in *Sister Carrie* : "Men are still led by instinct before they are regulated by knowledge. It is instinct which gives the criminal his feeling of danger, his fear of wrong."[38]

> Dreiser was firmly of the opinion that if a man were to replace his instincts by his free will he is going to suffer, not really benefit by it. We see man far removed from the lairs of the jungles, his innate instincts dulled by too near an approach to free will, his free-will not sufficiently developed to replace his instinct and afford him perfect guidance. He is becoming too wise to hearken always to instincts and desires; he is still weak to always prevail against them. As a beast, the force of life aligned him with them; as a man, he has not yet wholly learned to align himself with the forces. In this intermediate stage he wavers-neither drawn in harmony with nature by his instinct noryet wisely putting himself into harmony by his

> own free -will. He is even as a wisp in the wind, moved by every breath of passion, acting now by his will and now by his instincts, erring with one, only to retrieve by the other - a creature of incalculable variability.[39]

If a man were to follow his conscience, be guided by his instincts and work in alignment with nature, use money judiciously only for moral purposes and live with a spiritual affinity with the universe, then life would be worth living. Dreiser was quite confident in his belief that amidst all the working of Nature there was a definite plan or influence. In the introduction to a novel Giff, an account of a spiritualist, Dreiser has observed:

> In the face of all inductive science and the strange yet narrow walls of all naturalistic philosophies. . . . . I hold that behind the seemingly foolish predictions which "came true" moves something which is . . . solidly real. . an all pervasive intention or plan.[40]

The same idea is repeated in his "Introduction to Thoreau" where he feels that scientific knowledge will have to admit defeat because even though it can state how a thing happens, it cannot state why it happens and this is where God's or spirit's or *Brahma's* hand is at work.At this point one is reminded of Emerson's "Over soul", where there is a parallel to Dreiser's belief :

> We live in succession, division, in parts,in particles. Meantime within man is the soul of the whole; the wise silence; the universal beauty, to which every part and particle is equally related; the eternal ONE . . .We see the world piece by piece, as the sun, the moon, the animal, the tree; but the whole of which these are the shining parts, is the soul.[41]

Here Emerson is actually quoting ideas from *The Bhagavad Gita* and so does Dreiser. Henry David Thoreau also has similar lessons on spirituality for the reader. Thoreau in his essay "Where I lived And what I lived for" which is an extract from *Walden* has similar ideas on life. Thoroughly disagreeing with the theory that materialistic life brings pleasure, Thoreau insists that only a life of simplicity can produce real Happiness and that also only when man is ready to live in the present and not in the past or future.

> God himself culminates in the present moment, and will never be more divine in the lapse of all ages. And we are enabled to apprehend all what is sublime and noble only by the perpetual instilling and drenching of the reality that surrounds us. The universe constantly and obediently answers to our conceptions; whether we travel fast or slow, the track is laid for us. Let us spend our lives in conceiving them. [42]

In Nature a great storehouse of knowledge is freely available to us; only it needs a ready mind to perceive it and understand it. Dreiser's Naturalism, Realism and Darwinism are quite well known and appreciated.

Dreiser was actually looking for a scheme behind the apparent schemelessness or chaotic appearance of the universe. By delving into the mystery of the universe, Dreiser had come to understand, that selflessness, admiration of Beauty and appreciation of the unity in the scheme of things is what life is all about. Dudley has observed thus of Dreiser:

> he is an American high watermark, capable of waves that fall beyond. .. In him our disorderly order gleams with its mysteries. He says of himself, "The riddle remains. I have solved nothing.[43]

By saying that he has solved nothing, Dreiser is definitely being quite modest in his own assessment of himself. Philip Gerber's observation is that there is a gradual growth and understanding of the universe, as perceived by the novels.

From *Sister Carrie* to *The Stoic*, in this interpretation,

> Dreiser moved from his initial belief in the essential purposelessness of life toward the notionthat the exercise of ones will to power gave life meaning and zest, then moved from this espousal of rugged individualism towards a conversion to socialism that was allied with the belief that the evils of society can be ameliorated, and ended by surrendering to the powerful lure of the spirit.[44]

Sister Carrie's resolution to devote herself through her art to the betterment of all men and Berenice's achievement in accomplishing task of helping orphans and blind children are indeed Dreiser's own achievements in appreciating the fact that if each one does his little bit to help another, the whole universe would become a better place to live in.

Dreiser's novels were a revelation, they created an awareness in the minds of those who were allured by the American Dream of success. In *Sister Carrie*, there is a passage which cautions men from being unduly attached to visions of success " Not evil, but longing for that which is better, more often directs the steps of the erring. Not evil, but goodness more often allures the feeling mind unused to reason."[45]

Cautioning against indiscriminate desire, Dreiser has very emphatically presented the "passivity, rootlessness, and self alienation" of urban man. As Irving Howe has also observed Dreiser has pointed out that just as in his works the problem of human freedom becomes critically acute through a representation of its decline, so the problem of awareness is brought to the forefront through " a portrait of its negation." [46]

So, even though at the surface level or superficial level a novel like *An American Tragedy* seems to be showing the deterministic ideology as dragging the world along in its wake, but at a deeper level the novel's sustained reflection on the social and political effects of its own determinism stands as a form of resistance to that vision. According to Mizruchi that resistance reveals, above all, "a faith in human power to change the world." [47]

Dreiser's novels have thus been written with a purpose. *An American Tragedy* was sparked off by incidents such as the following:

> While working as a dishwasher in a fly specked restaurant one small group of employees did impress him, these were the scions of wealthy Easterners, monied Aristocrats came to study Western hardware methods and needs before returning as executive in their parents', establishments. These young men protected their smooth hands with gloves; under the denim collars of their work clothes one caught the gleam of silk shirts.[48]

Such a sight of luxury was despicable to Dreiser's eyes. He just could not tolerate and assimilate the fact while some were rolling in the lap of luxury others were to sweat it out for their daily bread. It was such incidents which made him write *An American Tragedy* forty years later but by then Dreiser had matured enough to understand that not envy and hatred of such people but an acceptance of the fact that such disparities do exist and a conscious effort in the rectification of it would actually improve his lot and not just sulking or feeling miserable about it. A few years later Dreiser understood that not succumbing to luxury but a resistance of it would enable a man to enjoy happiness without the fear of losing it.

Dreiser's *The Bulwark* has portrayed his mature vision of life. According to a lecture delivered by Philip Gerber at "American Studies Research Center" Hyderabad, in 1994, which I attended, Gerber's comment in a lecture was that *The Bulwark* is like "Bach Music", which waited long for full recognition. Many of Dreiser's concluding ideas are found here in "disarmingly simple form" .The whole book depicts a Quaker style of life and Dreiser has presented Quakerism "as a way which made strong Americans". These compel belief, fidelity and discipline-without which it would appear that man is not capable of leading a coherent life. The whole book asserts that man must be guided-that is, man in modern America- "by powerful attachments to an Authority that he accepts on faith."[49]

Dreiser had come to view that discipline is necessary to strengthen the will and make a spiritually stronger individual. Dreiser longed to be one even though personally he could never arrive at that state. A passage from *Hoosier Holiday* quoted by Burton Rascoe shows Dreiser's longing for such a blissful state.

> We Americans have home traditions or ideals, created as much by song and romance as anything else: My Old Kentucky Home, Swanee River. Despite any willing on my part, this home seemed to fulfill the spirit of those songs. There was something so sadly romantic about it. The shade of the great trees moved across the lawn in stately and lengthening curves..... Birds sang, and there were golden bees about the flowers and wasps under the eaves of the house... Ducks and geese solemnly paddled to and fro between the house and the stream. The air was redolent of corn,wheat, clover, timothy flowers.[50]

To him it seemed that all the spirit of rural America, its idealism, its dreams or the sadness of a Lincoln, the dreams and courage of a Lee or a Jackson were all there. The very soil smacked of American idealism and faith, a fixedness in sentimental and purely imaginative American tradition in which he could not share. He had seen Pittsburgh or the Lithuanians and Hungarians in their courts and novels. But the profound faith in God, in goodness, in virtue and duty which he saw in his Kentucky home was quite in contrast with the craft, the cruelty, the brutality and the envy that he saw every where else.

It was this ideal state of goodness and a duty bound spirit that Dreiser longed for and has also tried inculcating in his characters. This nobility, refinement and culture is what he was looking for, he felt that it was being diluted by man's selfishness. The following passage would definitely prove how the sensitive soul of Dreiser must have been affected by cruelty of human beings.

> Wild animals lived on men. And there were Indians and cannibals. And some men were killed by storms and

> accidents. He wasn't so sure about men living on men yet; but men did kill each other. He had seen a mob once. It attacked public ledger building as he was coming home from school. His father had explained what for, too. There was great excitement. It was about the slaves. That was it! Sure men lived on men. Look at the slaves. They were men. That's what all this excitement was about these days. Men killing other men -Negroes.[51]

These childhood impressions of Frank Cowperwood show how affected Dreiser was that he created the character of Cowperwood as a man striding over others only to have others stride over him during his old age. It is the humanitarianism in Dreiser that makes him project to what extent man can turn out to be cruel for his own selfish needs.

Dreiser's in depth study and questioning revealed to him the secret that only when man transcends beyond passions, desires and ambitions and accepted and acknowledged a oneness with one another and with Nature can one attain Peace and Happiness. As Etta has observed in *The Bulwark*:

> In this love and unity with all Nature, as she now sensed, there was nothing fitful or changing or disappointing that glowed one minute and was gone the next. This love was rather as constant as nature itself, everywhere the same, in sunshine or in darkness, the filtered splendour of the dawn, the seeded beauty of the night.It was an intimate relation to the very heart of being.[52]

In an article entitled "Kismat", Dreiser has observed thus:

> We are not permitted to decide, we have no freedom of thought or will. We do as the general mind.... Our reactions as well as the scene of condition to which we respond to or react are already arranged. We merely respond as we are instructed to respond, and not otherwise.[53]

Here Dreiser confirms his view that we are worked upon by the creative force and it directs our actions and he also believed that "The creative force that appears to operate directly through matter - energy as well as the laws and spatial conditions environing the same is, in fact, the one reality -universal creative reality."[54]

In a letter to Dorothy Payne Davis, Dreiser has himself stated that:

> All things to me are emanations and evolutions of cosmic forces and cosmic law. Buddha and Mary Baker Eddy affirmed an over Soul or one universal soul itself being and so containing all wisdom and all creative power l ly scientific as well as my philosophic studies compel me to feel that there can be but one primary creative force or soul.[55]

This letter clearly indicates that Dreiser while unravelling the mystery of the universe, had come to believe in the existence of a single creative force which was ruling and guiding the universe. In *Hey Rub-A-Dub-Dub* Dreiser's view is that "The nature of God, if not revealed by a voice of thunder from a mountain top, is, according to him, seen in the works of nature and the works of Nature are good."[56]

Dreiser's opinion is that nothing which is man-made is permanent and still we go making religions, law and rules on morality. All these are relative and they change with a change in society's views and style of living. The truth is that

> There remains only this necessity for equation, some form of adjustment,reciprocity, balance between the integral factor of each group, good, bad or indifferent, which no one thinks of translating as the only omnipresent evidence of so called Divine Will.[57]

Life is actually a series of adjustments so that some balance is maintained and life goes on. So the only thing permanent in this world is change, the one who readily and wisely adjusts to the change is the successful man. As Dreiser himself has pointed out in another essay "Change" :

> There is something controlling, or which we are a part and not a part; there is mystery to which we belong and yet which will not show to us its face. Only its impulses burst upon us from day to day and from century to century, making us weep from fear to regret, or faint with terror or thrill mild with joy. Out of the deeps they come , they brighten the face of its one outstanding tendency, which we must accept whether we will or not change.[58]

Having accepted this change no individuals can forcefully say

> God or the creator wishes us to do thus and so. We can only say that changing conditions compel us to or prevent us from doing thus and so. Nature may wish us to be forceful in many strange ways in order to that we may contest, bicker with other things equally forceful in other ways (all created by Her) so that out of the contest such as we may see, may come something which we can never see.[59]

Speaking in more detail on the same topic Dreiser wishes to make the reader understand:

> Our God, if we have one, is vast somewhat too great for the perception or understanding or destruction, or solution of any minor portion of Him, such as we are. He is a creator of spectacles, a slinger of thunder - bolts, a breather of fire, a master of cataclysm . . . No attributes such as man can conceive can apply. . . Our God is tragedy and comedy, terror and delight. He is limitless opportunity and endless opposition and destruction, for His way is extremes in equation, and nothing more and nothing less.[60]

This passage reminds one of a statement in the *Bhagavad Gita* wherein Lord Krishna states :

> I am the vedic ritual, I am the sacrifice,I am the offering to the departed, I am the medicinal herb, I am the sacred formula, I am the clarified butter, I am the sacred fire, and I am the act of offering oblation into the fire. I am the knowable, the purifier, the sacred syllable OM and the three Vedas... I am the father, sustainer, mother, grandfather, goal, supporter, lord,witness, abode refuge disinterested friend, origin, end, resting place,storehouse and the imperishable seed of this universe.[61]

So if everything is preconceived and if we are only acted upon, then should man say that life is limited and there is no opportunity for progress? Dreiser feels that it is not necessary for man to weep but to continue striving to make it world because a better place just as plants, trees or flowers do. They do not waste their energy thinking that they might not exist tomorrow and stop growing or flowering. So also man should carry on with life's activities and may be become a Shakespeare or Alexander or Hannibal according to his abilities and mental make up.

> What, then, shall man do?...Shall he say that it (life) is limited, that there is no opportunity for progress, or that the sweetness of those things defined as love, charity, mercy, neighborliness and race sociability are by such a governing condition destroyed. Not at all. Wherein is the temperament of Nature Herself, Her sweetness, if such there be; Herromance,.... Her beauty,.... altered by this? [62]

Men need to have a cosmic understanding and compassion for one's fellow beings and a readiness to part with a portion of, wealth in order to support some other unfortunate being is recommended by Dreiser . The passage in *Sister Carrie* where a soldier stands collecting money for putting some unfortunate out - of -work creatures to bed is reminiscent of the Biblical saying which considers duty towards one's fellowmen as duty towards God. The condition of the unfortunate creatures is quite pathetic.

> One might see, now, some of the chief characteristics by contrast. There was a wooden leg in the line...drooping trousers were all warped and frayed at the bottom and coats worn and faded. In the glare of the store lights,some of the faces looked dry and chalky; others were red with blotches and puffed in the cheeks and under the eyes; one or two were raw boned and reminded one of railroad hands....[63]

It is these pathetic and unfortunate men who need support and patronage and the soldier who aided them in getting a bed was almost a God incarnate to those miserable men. According to F.O.Mathiessen Dreiser's view was that "virtue is that quality of generosity which offers itself willingly for another's service."[64]

A liberal attitude towards fellow creatures would make all men feel accepted and the void or loneliness created in their minds by misery, starvation and disease would be relieved. Therefore Dreiser had conceived of a God who could be anything from "Brahma" , "Vital Force" , "Universe" or "Mind" who transcends all human beings and alleviates suffering by guiding man in the path to Universal Happiness.Scientific advancement had somehow made Americans as well as all human beings so complacent and self - centered that Dreiser's novels are a call to humanity to rise out of the spiritual awakening and make man more and more humble and philanthropic, instead of resorting to craftiness and cruelty. If all men could unite they could definitely shape a better destiny for not only all human beings but all God's creations on earth.The following passage from *Hey Rub-A-Dub-Dub* elucidates Dreiser's compassion for all creatures on earth.

> The song of ultimate perfection continues yearly , from century to century, to be sung. The divine, far-off event (which, if anything, is Nirvana) is surely coming Man is to be saved from hunger,cold, thirst, lust, undue

> material ambition, by telling him how horrible they are and asking him to be kind. ...For behold -man himself is superimposed upon other forms of life and thrives only by their destruction. Do you suppose the ox, the hog, the horse, the fish man slays or enslaves in order that he may be comfortable could be made to look upon him as tender, merciful....[65]

The answer would be a definite No. So man can be known to be merciful if he lives in harmony with Nature without intruding in or disturbing others lives for his own selfish needs. An unobtrusive, harmless policy with tenderness and love for all could only create HEAVEN on earth .

Even as a child, Dreiser was quite affectionate towards his family and friends. He was a sensitive artist with a keen eye for meticulous perfection and a lover of beauty wherever it was revealed in women, art or nature . To some extent Eugene represented Dreiser who also admired beauty and had a weakness for beautiful women. After years of admiring natural and physical beauty Dreiser took to admiring spiritual beauty in *The Bulwark* and the beauty of sharing and being philanthropic in *The Stoic*.So gradually Dreiser is drawn from external to internal beauty of the spirit and ultimately identifies beauty in the service of others. Eugene Witla's exclamation at the end of the novel is Dreiser's own feeling. "Life, at bottom, in spite of all its teeming terror, was beautiful."[66]

Dreiser's heart was always with the wretched, the miserable, the underdog of society. In an appeal made to other writers in Nov. 1933 he has made a clarion call to fellow Americans to join together to make a better America. " Join Now. write, speak, entertain, struggle for and with those whose future is your future."[67]

This appeal holds good to all humanity and not only to the community of writer, because if all were to follow them we could create a better social order.At this point I am reminded of an appeal made by Adi Shankaracharya in his *Bhaja Govindam*

> Moodha Jaheehi Dhanagama trishnam
> Kuru sadbudhim Manasi Vithrishnam
> Yallabhase Nijakarmop patham
> Vitham Tena Vinodhaya Chitam [68](Bhaja Govindam.......)

[Oh Fool! Give up the thirst to possess wealth. Create in your mind, devoid of passions, thoughts of the reality. With whatever you get (as a reward of the past), entertain your mind (be content). (Seek Govind)]

Man has definitely been created on earth with a purpose, so he has to realize it, aspire for it and try to achieve it. There's no point whiling away one's precious time in sensuous and purposeless expeditions. Having realized one's goal if one can proceed towards it with dedication and a sense of responsibility in a humble manner shall one attain a state of Perfection.

Dreiser had also developed this faith that only a purposeful existence with single minded devotion and dedication can transport man towards achievement of nirvana or the essence of life. The only fault in human life is that instead of working for the benefit of society as a whole, we are all busy thinking of the immediate benefits and that is why we fail.

In the novel *Financier* , Dreiser has pointed out that materialism cannot guarantee an ideal state of living.

> A Christian ideal has been poured out upon the world like a sea of air, and those who live in it, who are many, draw their convictions as their breath from that something underneath the flesh,for instance, and material pleasure - was against it; but it is almost a part of their blood, so long has the world moved in it. Still the native materiality of man will not drown any more than his ideality.Perhaps the two go hand in hand. Before Christianity was man, and after it he will also be. A metaphysical idealism will

> always tell him that it is better to preserve a cleanly balance, and the storms of circumstances will teach him a noble stoicism. Beyond this there is nothing which can reasonably be imposed upon the conscience of man.[69]

We find that in life there are many ways in which our life is regulated or streamlined. Many occurrences remind us of the facility of being self centered but still it is surprising that some individuals just cling on to their haphazard way of living with no conscience whatsoever to regulate their lives. "We see much punishment in the form of jails, diseases, failures and wrecks; but we also see that the old tendency is not visibly lessened. Is there no law outside of the subtle will and power to achieve?"[70]

The answer to this question posed by Dreiser regarding the mystery of the universe is found in a subsequent chapter in *The Financier,*

> I am no spiritualist, nor theosophist, but this gift ,or occasional visitation of providence, or whatever else people may choose to call it, to which I am subject at intervals, has saved me from being financially shattered at least two or three times every year I have known others who have had these mysterious forebodings but who recklessly disregarded them; and this has been the rock on which they have split in speculative emergencies.[71]

If businessmen can have such warnings of ill luck or whatsoever they would definitely have warnings of being over - materialistic also. It only needs a prepared mind to understand this philosophy and then there would not be so much distress or disturbance in the whole world. Such psychic or psychological intuitions occur as guiding spirits or warnings. If human beings are ready to be guided then one can control one's excessive desires.

Depressed by the variety of methods used by individuals to trick or dupe one another Dreiser has insisted that all this chicanery and trickery is only Maya and the sooner we perceive this the better.

Dreiser has explained this fact with a beautiful imagery taken from Nature:

> Mycteroperca moving in its dark world of green waters is as fine an illustration of the constructive genius of nature. Its great superiority lies in an almost unbelievable power of simulation which relates solely to the pigmentation of its skin..... You cannot look at it for long without feeling that you are witnessing something spectral and unnatural, so brilliant is its power to deceive. From being black it can become instantly white; from being an earth coloured brown it can fade into a delicious water coloured green. Its markings change as the clouds of the sky. One marvels at the variety and subtlety of its power.[72]

Some men also change colours as quickly as this creature. But all this chicanery and trickery are to lead man nowhere as he would ultimately be won over by someone more powerful than him. Therefore it is an illusion. There are other beautiful occurrences of Nature referred by Dreiser of how insects trap victims. Dreiser has pointed out how

> The horrific spider spinning its trap for the unthinking fly; the lovely Drosera(Sundew) using its crimson calyx for a smothering -pit in which to seal and devour the victim of its beauty; the rainbow- coloured jelly fish that spreads its prismed tentacles like streamers of great beauty, only to sting and torture all that falls within their radiant folds.Man himself is busy digging the pit and fashioning the snare, but he will not believe it. His feet are in the trap of circumstance, his eyes are on an illusion. [73]

This world of illusion or Maya as the Hindus term it is only drawing mankind further and further away from reality. The sooner we realize it, the better, for, we can at least hope to be resurrected before being doomed forever. So Dreiser's sincere advice is to follow the paths of pity and affection. Regarding affection Dreiser has observed that all human beings definitely have an affectionate feeling, a feeling of tenderness towards one's kith and kin.

> The world wanders into many strange by - paths of affection. The love of a mother for her children is dominant, leonine,selfish and unselfish. It is Concentric.The love of a husband for his wife, or of a lover for his sweetheart, is a sweet bond of agreement and exchange......The love of a father for his son or daughter where it is love at all, is a broad,generous; sad, contemplative giving without thought of return, a hail and farewell to a troubled traveller whom he would do much to guard, a balanced judgement of weakness or strength, with pity for failure and pride in achievement.It is a lovely, generous, philosophic blossom which rarely asks too much, and seeks only to give wisely and plentifully.[74]

If the world could adopt this sort of love -especially the last type, that of father for son- towards one another then there would no place for unhappiness -only the dawning of the realization that we are all atoms of the same Universal spirit is needed, and then there would be Heaven on Earth. Regarding pity or compassion for one another, Dreiser's observations are as follows:-

> Let no one underestimate the need of pity. We live in a stony universe whose hard, brilliant forces rage fiercely. From the prowling hunger of the Hyrcan tiger to the concentric grip of Arcturus and Canopus there is this same ruthless, sightless disregard of the individual and the minor thing. Life moves in an ordered hierarchy of forces of which the lesser is as nothing to the greater. And in the midst of the rip of desperate things -in odd crannies and chance flaws between forces there spring and bloom these small flowers of sentiment. Tenderness! Mercy! Affection! Sorrow! Blessed are the merciful, for they shall receive mercy!No, no. Blessed are the merciful, for they create me. Of such is the kingdom of the ideal.[75]

Herein Dreiser stresses that the ability to feel pity and be compassionate is a very rare, unique quality and therefore it should be cultivated because "tenderness" , "mercy" , "affection" and so on are essentially human gifts and ones which differentiate us from the world of animals and show us to be more sensitive to one another's joys and sorrows.

Dreiser's observation in *Hey Rub-A-Dub-Dub* is that unfortunately the common man was quite unsure of the meaning and implication the words, "truth, mercy, justice."

> In the main it seems to me that people are not concerned about right, or truth, or justice, or mercy, or duty, as abstract principles or working rules, do I believe that the average man knows clearly or semi clearly what is meant by these words. His only relation to them is that he finds them used in a certain reckless, thoughtless way to represent some method of adjustment by which he would like to think he is protected from assault or saved from misery, and so uses them himself.[76]

So even if men use such words it is without a clear perception of what it underlines. The question of adapting these attitudes sensibly and sensitively with an intention of uplifting or elevating one another's lives is out of question. This attitude is highly destructive and rather divesting. We were not created for this purpose. So its high time people started questioning the mystery of creation and strived to arrive at an answer.In a quotation in his "Every Month" column Dreiser has observed as how men should behave:

> All must die that [man] may live -fruits,flowers, animals and vegetables. The very hills must be torn to give him homes of stone, and the forests destroyed that he may have the beauty of ornamental carving about him. He must step in where others have failed, crowd out the old and feeble,override the desires and hopes of others who also wish for success, and so on, until death. This is the law, cold, hard,immutable the law of self - preservation and

> upon it all must take their stand and press forward so or die. It is hard to think that such must be the condition of living, but nevertheless, such it must be and all honor to him who fights bravest but with as much charity and as many tears as the dread of failure will permit.[77]

The point to be noted is that while fighting to preserve oneself in this world full of struggle, one should not forget the fact that one should also live for others in whatever small way one can and also one should be charitable and sympathetic towards one's environment. It is not wealth, power, luxury or influence which will contribute to human happiness, but " a speck of human kindness in the sea of need and despair is what would work wonders with the world."[78]

Berenice of the trilogy achieved utmost satisfaction while serving two small blind children who had in some way, got into her ward. They had been blind from birth. One, was a small frail blond child of five years named Patricia. She was a daughter of a hard working girl who had no time for her child, had been allowed to sit for hours in a little rocking chair in a corner, with not the least stimuli or interest. When Berenice found this "isolated mite of humanity", she became fascinated by her and desired to help her, teaching her many little things, among them being how to slide with confidence down a chute in the children's court. So much joy had Patricia experienced from this simple stunt, that she did this over and over again for hours, each time "radiating with happiness at her newly found independence."[79] This joy which one can infuse in the hearts of the deprived, the sick, the ignorant, the grief stricken is what life is all about. It is not from a "socially secure position"[80] but from a "socially worthwhile vocation" that Berenice found job satisfaction and a sense of achievement. A peace that surpasses understanding occurs while serving others because:

> Part of myself is the God within
> every creature, keeps that nature eternal,
> yet seems to be separate,
> Putting on mind and senses five, the garment
> Mode of Prakriti.[81]

So in the course of his novels beginning with *Sister Carrie* and *Jennie Gerhardt,* moving on to the trilogy and ending with *The Stoic* and *The Bulwark* , Dreiser has tried to erase out of the American mind the unnatural obsession with material advancement. He has made a call to humanity to explore how Cosmic Consciousness, a Oneness with Nature and a philanthropic and magnanimous mind, ready to help others in distress, can bring about Universal Peace, Contentment and a Sense of Accomplishment and Fulfillment in society.

Thus Dreiser's "Quest For Belief" ended with his perception of Oneness and harmony between Nature, and between all the elements, objects and living beings in the Universe. He established his firm faith in a Just, Lovely and Supremely Resourceful and Powerful Force or Being who creates and carries the Universe, on, towards its destiny.

NOTES AND REFERENCES

[1]John Mc Aleer, *Theodore Dreiser: An Introduction and Interpretation*,(New York: Holt, 1968),1.

[2]William J.Fisher, *American Literature of the Nineteenth Century* (New Delhi: Eurasia Publishing House, 1980),97.

[3]Swami Ramsukhdas , *Sadhaka Sanjivani (* Gorakhpur :Geeta Press),539.

[4]Swami Ramsukhdas , *Sadhaka Sanjivani*,540.

[5]Swami Ramsukhdas , *Sadhaka Sanjivani*,541.

[6]Pfizer, *The Novels of Theodore Dreiser*,371.

[7]HariKrishanadasGoyanka,*IshovadinoUpanishad*(Gorakhpur:Gita Press),93.

[8]Walt Whitman, Song of Myself Sec. 20 line 391 ,*An Anthology of American Litt. of the 19th Century* 320.

[9]Dreiser, *The Stoic*,295.

[10]Shri Shankaracharya, *Bhaja Govindam with commentary by Swami Chinmayananda* (Madras: Chinmaya Publications Trust, 1977),21.

[11]Dreiser, *Hey Rub-A-Dub-Dub*,218.

[12]Tjader, *Dreiser: A New Dimension*,127.

[13]Dreiser, "Introduction" *Theodore Dreiser Presents the Living Thoughts of Thoreau,* (New York: Longmans Green & Co.,1939),2.

[14]Dreiser, *Moods* (New York, 1935),316.

[15]Dreiser, *Tragic America*,202.

[16]Dreiser, *Tragic America*,84.

[17]Dreiser, *To the Russian People*(Jan 13, 1928).

[18]Dreiser, *Tragic America*,247.

[19]Dreiser, *Dawn*,197.

[20]Dreiser, *An Amateur Labourer* (Philadelphia: Univ. of Pennyslvania Press,1983),85.

[21]Dreiser, *Hey Rub-A-Dub-Dub*,266-267.

[22]Dreiser, *The Titan*,552.

[23]Dreiser, *Sister Carrie*,252.

[24]Dreiser, *Notes on Life* (The Salve called Religion),278.

[25]Swami Ramsukhdas, *Sadhaka Sanjivani*,501.

[26]Dreiser, *Sister Carrie*,254.

[27]Swanberg, *Dreiser,*176.

[28]Dorothy Dudley, *Dreiser and the Land of the Free* (New York: Harrison Smith, 1932),471-72.

[29]Dreiser, *The Genius,*418.

[30]Dreiser, *Tragic America,*3.

[31]Dreiser, *Tragic America,*30.

[32]Dreiser, *Tragic America,*109.

[33]Dreiser, *Tragic America,*112.

[34]Dreiser, *Hey Rub-A-Dub-Dub,*255-256.

[35]Dreiser, *Hey Rub-A-Dub-Dub,*257.

[36]Tjader,*Dreiser. A New Dimension,*176.

[37]Dreiser,*A Book About Myself*(New York: 1965) 589.

[38]Dreiser, *Sister Carrie(*New York: Doubleday. Page.1900), 286-287.

[39]Dreiser, *Sister Carrie,*83.

[40]Sidney Richman, *Critical Essays of Theodore Dreiser Ed. by Pfizer* (Boston: G.K. Hall & Co., 1981),324.

[41]Fisher Samuelson& Reminger Vaid, *An Anthology of American Literature of the Nineteenth Century* (New Delhi: Chand & Co.,1980),84.

[42] - Samuelson & Reminger Vaid, *An Anthology of American Literature of the Nineteenth Century*, 146.

[43]Dudley,*Dreiser and the Land of the Free* 3-4.

[44]Gerber, *Theodore Dreiser Revisited,*129.

[45]Dreiser, *Sister Carrie* (New York: Airmont Publishing Co., 1967},381.

[46]Irving Howe, Afterword to American Tragedy, 826.

[47]Mizruchi,*The Power of Historical Knowledge* 294.

[48]Gerber,*Theodore Dreiser Revisited* ,34-35.

[49]Walcutt, *American Literary Naturalism,*219.

[50]Rascoe Burton, *Theodore Dreiser* (New York: Mcbride, 1925), 26-27.

[51]Dreiser, *The Financier* U.S.A: Harper and Brothers,1912), 14.

[52]Dreiser , *The Bulwark* ,331.

[53]Dreiser, Kismat, Esquire III, I(Jan. 1935),29175-176.

[54]Dreiser, The Mechanism called Man (n.d.). U.P.

[55]Theodore Dreiser to Dorothy Payne Davis July 18, 1940-41.

[56]Dreiser, *Hey Rub-A-Dub-Dub*,159.

[57]Dreiser, *Hey Rub-A-Dub-Dub*,160.

[58]Dreiser, *Hey Rub-A-Dub-Dub*, 22-23.

[59]Dreiser, *Hey Rub-A-Dub-Dub*,162.

[60]Dreiser, *Hey Rub-A-Dub-Dub*,81.

[61]Swami Ramsukhdas, *Srimad BhagavadGita* Ch. IX Verses 16,17,18.

[62]Dreiser, *Hey Rub-A-Dub-Dub*,177-178.

[63]Dreiser, *Sister Carrie*,356.

[64]F.O.Mathiessen, *Theodore Dreiser*{London: Mathiessen & Co..1951),121.

[65]Dreiser, *Hey Rub-A-Dub-Dub*,167-168.

[66]Dreiser, *The Genius*,695.

[67]Dreiser, Challenge to the creative man Common Sense. II (Nov.1933),7-8.

[68]Bhagwan Shri Shankaracharya.*Bhaja Govindam* (Madras, India: Hoe & Co., 1977),13.

[69]Dreiser, *The Financier*,250.

[70]Dreiser, *The Financier*,254.

[71]Dreiser, *The Financier*,414-415.

[72]Dreiser, *The Financier*,778-779.

[73]Dreiser, *The Financier*,778.

[74]Dreiser, *The Financier*,363.

[75]Dreiser, *The Financier*,409-410.

[76]Dreiser, *Hey Rub-A-Dub-Dub*,6-7.

[77]Pfizer, *The Novels of Theodore Dreiser*,13.

[78]Dreiser, *The Stoic*,309.

[79]Dreiser, *The Stoic*,308-309.

[80]Dreiser, *The Stoic*,309.

[81]Dreiser, *The Stoic*,275.

Select Bibliography

Books by Dreiser

Novels

Sister Carrie.NewYork:Airmont Publishing Co.,1967.

Jennie Gerhardt. Britain: O.U.P, 1992.

The Financier. New York: Harper, 1912.

The "Genius" . New York: John Lane and Co. , 1915.

An American Tragedy. New York:Signet Classic, New American Library 1981.

The Bulwark Garden City, New York: Doubleday,1946.

The Stoic. Garden City, New York: Doubleday, 1947.

Autobiography and Travel Account

A Traveler at Forty. New York: Century, 1923.

A Hoosier Holiday. New York: John Lane, 1916.

A Book About Myself. NewYork: Boni and Liveright,1922.

Dreiser Looks at Russia.New York:H.Liveright, 1928.

Dawn. New York: H.Liveright, 1931.

Poets

Moods, Cadenced and Declaimed. New York: Simon and Schuster,1935.

Plays

Plays of the Natural and the Supernatural. NewYork: John Lane, 1916.

Short Stories

Free, and Other Stories. New York: Boni and Liveright, 1918.

Chains. New York: Boni and Liveright, 1927.

The Best Short Stories. ed. James T.Farvell,Greenwich, Conn.,Fawcett, 1956.

Fulfillment and Other Tales of Women and Men. Ed. T.D. Nostwich, Santa Rosa:Black Sparrow Press, 1992

Non Fiction

Twelve Men. New York: Boni and Liveright 1919.

Hey Rub-A-Dub-Dub! .New York:Boni and Liveright, 1920.

The Color of A Great City. New York: Boni and Liveright, 1923.

A Gallery of Women. New York: Boni and Liveright, 1929.

Tragic America. New York: Boni and Liveright, 1931.

America in Worth Saving. New York: Modern Age Books, 1911.

An Amateur Laborer. Philadelphia: Univ. of Pennyslvania, 1983.

Letters

Letters of Theodore Dreiser ed. with preface and notes by Robert H.Elias.Philadelphia: University of Pennyslvania Press, 1959 (3 Vols.).

Dreiser-Mencken Letters ed. Thomas P.Riggio Philadelphia: University of Pennyslvania Press, 1986.

Dreiser to Sinclair, December 18, 1924; Lilly Library, Indiana University.

Introductions

"Introduction" , *Harlan Miners Speak*, New York: Harcourt, Brace and Company, 1932.

"Introduction" , *Theodore Dreiser Presents the Living Thoughts of Thoreau-* New York:Longmans, Green and Co.,1939.

Articles

"What I Believe".*The Forum,* LXXXII (Nov. 1929), 279-281.

"The Child and the School".*The American Spectator,*I (April 1933),2.

"The Myth of Individuality". *The American Mercury,* XXXI (March 1934).

"What to do?" .*Free World,* IX (March 1945),10(Poem).

"Interdependence" .*Free World,* X (September 1945), 69-70.

Notes on Life. Ed. by Marguerite Tjader and John Mc. Aleer, Univ. of Alabama Press, 1974.

Criticism on Dreiser

Bowlby, Rachel. *Just Looking: Consumer Culture in Dreiser, Gissing and Zola,* New York: Methuen, 1985.

Charles Shapiro Ed. *Twelve Original Essays On Great American Novels,* Detroit: Wayne State University Press, 1958.

Davis, David Brion. "Dreiser and Naturalism Revisited" , *The stature of Theodore Dreiser.* Eds. Alfred Kazin and Charles Shapiro. Bloomington: Indiana University Press, 1958.

Dreiser, Helen. *My Life With Dreiser.* Cleveland, Ohio World, 1951.

Dudley, Dorothy. *Forgotten Frontiers: Dreiser and*

the Land of the free.New York: Harrison Smith, 1932.

Elias, Robert H. *Theodore Dreiser: Apostle of Nature.* Ithaca: Cornell University Press, 1971.

----. *Theodore Dreiser: Apostle of Nature*, New York: knopf,1949.

Fecher, Charles A., Knopf, Alfred A. Foreword Mencken: A Study of his Thought. New York: Knopf, 1978

Ford, Ford Madox. Portraits from Life: Memories and Criticism Chicago: Regnery Gateway, 1961.

Frohock, Wilbur Merrill. Theodore Dreiser Minneapolis Univ. of Minnesota Press, 1972.

Gerber, Philip L. Theodore Dreiser Revisited. Ed. by Joseph M. Flora.Univ. of North Carolina, New York: Twayne Publishers, 1992.

----. Plots and Characters in The Fiction of Theodore Dreiser Hamden, CONN: Shoe String, 1977.

Geismar, Maxwell. American Moderns. From Rebellion Conformity.New York: Hill and Wang, 1958.

Goyanka Hari Krishandas. Ishovadino Upanishad.(India) Gorakhpur: Gita Press.

Griffin Joseph. The Small Canvas: An Introduction to Dreiser's Short Stories. Rutherford, N.J.: Dickinson Univ. Press, 1985.

Hakutani, Yoshinobu. Young Dreiser: A Critical Study. Rutherford: Fairleigh Dickinson Univ. Press, 1980.

Handy, Willram J. Modern Fiction: A Formalist Approach

Carbondale: Southern Illinois University Press, 1971

Hussman, Lawrence E. Dreiser And His Fiction: A Twentieth Century Quest. Philadephia: University of Pennyslvania Press, 1983 .

John Mc. Aleer. Theodore Dreiser: An Introduction and Interpretation. New York: Holt, 1968.

Kar, P.C and Ramakrishna,D.Eds. The American Classics Revisited Hyderabad; ASRC, 1984.

Kazin, Alfred Ed, Shapiro Charles, Ed. The Stature of Theodore Dreiser: A Critical Survey of the Man and His Work. Bloomington: Indiana University Press, 1965.

Kennell, Ruth Epperson. Theodore Dreiser and the Soviet Union. New York: International Publishers, 1969.

Laskey, Melvin J. Ed. Anchor Review. No.1 Garden City, N.Y. Doubleday, 1955.

Lingeman, Richard R. Theodore Dreiser. New York: Putnam, 1986.

Lundquit, James. Theodore Dreiser. New York: Ungar, 1974.

Lynn, Kenneth S. The Dream of Success: A Study of The Modern American Imagination. Boston: Little, 1955.

Madden, David. Eight Classic American Novels San Diego: Harcourt Brace Jovanowich, 1990 .

Matthiessen, F.O: The American Men of Letters Series : Theodore Dreiser New York: Dell Publishing Co. Mar. 1966.

Maxwell, D.E.S. American Fiction: The Intellectual Background. London: Routledge and Kegan Paul, 1963.

Mencken, H.L. A Book of Prefaces. New York: Knopf., 1922.

Millgate, Michael. American Social Fiction: James to Cozzens. New York: Barnes. 1964 .

Moers, Ellen. Two Dreisers. New York: Viking Press, 1969.

Mookerjee R.N. Theodore Dreiser, His Thought and Social Criticism. Delhi: National Publishers, 1974.

Morgan, Howard Wayne. American Writers In Rebellion From Mark Twain to Dreiser. New York: Hill and Wang.

Mukherjee, Arun. Gospel of Wealth in the American Novel: Rhetoric of Dreiser and some of His

Contemporaries . London: Croom Helm, 1987.

Oatwalt, Conrad Eugene. After Eden: The secularisation of American Space in the Fiction of Willa Cather and Theodore Dreiser.Lewisburg PA: Associated University Press, 1990 .

Pfizer, Donald. Critical Essays on Theodore Dreiser. Boston, Mass: G.K.Hall and Co., 1981.

----. The Novels of Theodore Dreiser: Minneapolis: University of Minnesota Press, 1976 .

Raja, L. Jeganatha. Theodore Dreiser: Apostle of Nature. New York: Knopf., 1949.

Rascoe, Burton. Prometheans, Ancient and Moderns. New York Putnam 1933 .

Richard, Lehan. Theodore Dreiser: His World and His Novels. Carbondale: Southern Illinois University Press, 1969.

Salzman, Jack. Ed. Theodore Dreiser: The Critical Reception- New York: David Lewis, 1972.

Samueleon Fisher and Vaid Reninger .Eds. An Anthology: American Literature of the Nineteenth Century Ram Nagar, New Delhi: Eurasia Publishing House, 1964 .

Shri Shankaracharya Bhaja Govindam. Madras: Chinmaya Publications, 1977.

Spencer, Herbert. First Principles. New York, 1886.

Spiller, Robert E. et al. Eds. "Theodore Dreiser" Literary History of the United States. New York: The Macmillan Co., 1948.

Swami Ramsukhdas . Sadhaka Sanjivani .(India) Gorakhpur: Gita Press.

Swanberg, W.A. Theodore Dreiser. U.S.A: Bantam books Inc., March 1967 .

Takashimo, Atsuko. Essays And Studies in British and American Literature. Vol. I, No.1, 1959.

Takeda, Miyoko. The Quest For the Reality of life: Dreiser's Spiritual and Esthetical Pilgrimage. New York: Peter Lang, 1991.

Tjader, Marguerite Theodore Dreiser: A New Dimension. Norwalk, Conn.: Silvermine, 1965.

Vivas, Eliseo. Creation and Discovery: Essays in Criticism and Aesthetics. New York: Noonday Press, 1955.

Vivekananda. The Computer Works of Swami Vivekananda, Nols. I and II. Calcutta: Advaita Ashrama1976

Walcutt, Charles Child. American Literary Naturalism: A Divided

Stream. Minneapolis: University of Minnesota Press., 1956

West, James L.W. A Sister Carrie Portfolio. Charlottesville: University Press of Virginia 1985

Whipple, Thomas King. Spokesman: Modern Writers and American Life. New York: Appleton, 1928

Zola, Emile. The Natural Novel. Ed. with an introduction By Maxwell Geismar. Montreal: Harvest House, 1964

INDEX